I0479841

35* Disturbing Stories™ about the Veterans Administration™

*because I had to stop somewhere

by

A Concerned Veteran™

© 2020, A Concerned Veteran

Please attribute all quotes.
Thank You.

5 Disturbing Facts™ 35 Disturbing Stories™ and subsequent
Disturbing titles are trademarks owned by A Concerned Veteran.

Please direct all inquiries to:
shutdowntheva@gmail.com

Together, we can do this. ™

Thank you

Each of the sources cited in this publication is doing a great service for their country by allowing the use/reprint of their stories in this publication.

The military are not the only ones that risk their lives in war. To keep you informed, journalists are also on the front lines of conflicts, here and on foreign soil. Support journalism and your local journalist.

ShutDownTheVA@gmail.com

Who Am I?

I am a veteran. I am ill.

Part of what will kill me was caused by malpractice at the Veterans Administration.

Another part of what will kill me is from the effects of Agent Orange. Yes, it is really bad stuff.

Here are my goals:
1. The first goal is to stop the abuse of veterans at Veterans Affairs medical facilities.
2. The second goal is to shut down the VA and re-open it away from the bureaucratic hands of the government, which should not be in the business of running hospitals.

I remain anonymous because my name is not important. The issues are important. Veteran healthcare is important.

Thank you for reading.

ShutDownTheVA@gmail.com

Links

When reading this on Kindle or other electronic device, hyperlinks are turned on. What this means is that the online version of this book has <u>underlined</u> words or phrases that can take you to the original source of the article or supply more information about a topic when selected by clicking.

I have taken every precaution to ensure each link to be safe. But nothing is forever. So be cautious when browsing or clicking on links. Links provided here are not a guarantee that you are browsing safely.

Understand the need for secure browsing before taking chances. If you have software installed to help you detect phishing or malware, don't ignore warmings. And if you receive a message saying a website is not secure, don't go there.

I assume no legal liability for adverse consequences of your internet usage.

ShutDownTheVA@gmail.com

Dedication

This book of stories is dedicated to the memory of my fellow veterans who took their own lives. I promise to continue to fight for a safe and trusting healthcare system for military veterans. You will not be forgotten.

ShutDownTheVA@gmail.com

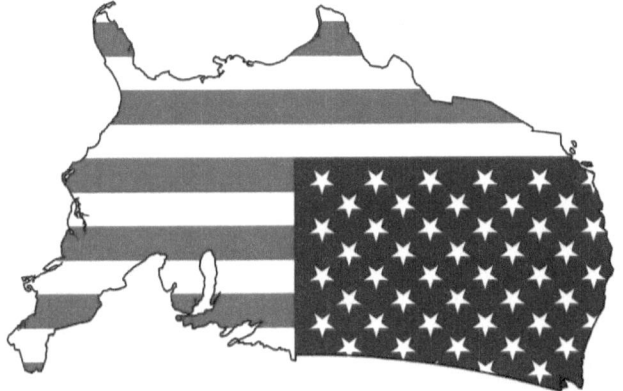

ShutDownTheVA@gmail.com

Table of Contents

ShutDownTheVA@gmail.com

ShutDownTheVA@gmail.com

ShutDownTheVA@gmail.com

ShutDownTheVA@gmail.com

ShutDownTheVA@gmail.com

ShutDownTheVA@gmail.com

ShutDownTheVA@gmail.com

Introduction

On the title page of this book, I place an asterisk by the book title and a link that states, "because I had to stop somewhere."

It's a flippant remark, for sure. But it's also true. I am not authoring this book because there have been 10 or 100 or 500 problems at the VA over the past 100 years. I am writing this book because there are thousands upon thousands of stories about the problems at the Veterans Administration. If you don't believe me, search the internet for yourself.

These stories are everywhere. And it's not about failure to treat ingrown toenails or a tooth that abscessed. Because of the internet we can now piece together the sham of healthcare at the Veterans Administration through the decades, by researching newspapers, magazines and blogs, all of which detail bad experiences at the VA, including cases of malpractice, abuse and even death.

Indeed, what you have heard on the news or read about in the newspaper is, but a small sample of what veterans face each day when they trust their healthcare to this secretive government agency.

ShutDownTheVA@gmail.com

It's a crisis.

How bad is it? It's a crisis. It's a national shame.

How often during the past 50 years has the public heard promises to "fix" the Veterans Administration.?

And how often, after hearing these promises, did you hear about another VA scandal? And again. And again.

And then we hear the same promises to "fix" it again.

My fellow Americans, you are being lied to.

The systemic deficiencies at the Veterans Administration run deep. So deep that not even the politicians understand how bad it is. And who do they rely on to tell them how the VA is working? The VA, of course. They rely on bureaucrats, bean counters and career federal employees who purposefully perpetuate this inept system of healthcare running so they can protect their jobs.

The Veterans Are Suffering

Our nations veterans are being abused. They are dying. They are being crippled and maimed. Sometimes accidentally by poorly trained staff and sometimes intentionally by malicious staff who retaliate against veterans for complaining.

ShutDownTheVA@gmail.com

Save Our VA

These bureaucrats at the VA are so worried that they will be discovered that they infiltrated veterans' groups with promises and a slogan campaign called "Save Our VA".

They are hoping to convince veterans that they are getting world class healthcare. They want to convince veterans that mean people are trying to steal their healthcare away from them.

Nothing could be further from the truth.

In fact, quite the opposite is true. It has become common knowledge among Washington insiders that the VA is not worth saving in its current form. It's not being said publicly, yet, but the changes are being developed.

But the changes to the Veterans Administration that are being planned are not enough. Why? Because the only way to fix healthcare for veterans once and for all is to take healthcare away from the government and fund it through a public non-profit that includes veteran and citizen oversight committees.

It's the only way to save veteran's lives.

ShutDownTheVA@gmail.com

A Challenge to Veterans

I challenge each veteran to become more active in their healthcare. Do the following and if you are not convinced that something is very wrong at the Veterans Administration, then I will withdraw all of my publications. Here's what I want you to do:

1. Ask for your medical records. Make sure you ask for *everything*, including the files being kept on you in VISTA.
2. Before you have a procedure,
    a. Ask to see a paper copy of the consent form.
    b. Read it before you sign it.
    c. If you don't agree with something you read, or don't understand it, ask questions.
    d. Do not sign anything until you understand everything you are agreeing to have performed.
    e. Get a copy of the consent form you sign before leave your appointment.
    f. After a procedure is performed, get your medical records and read them. Was everything done during the procedure that you agreed to? Was something done that you didn't agree to?
    g. Are there names in the records that you don't recognize? Ask who they are.
3. Ask questions during your appointments.
    a. Ask the doctors experience with your condition.

        b. Ask if your "doctor" is a doctor or is he/she a resident? A P.A."

        c. Request the same doctor for each visit.

4. Find out who the Privacy Officer is for the facility where you are treated.

        a. Write a letter to the Privacy Officer stating you wish to rescind the sharing of your medical records with anyone without your written permission for each person and each instance.

        b. Wait for the reply. Read it. Were you denied?

5. Do these 4 things and you'll be questioning that "Save Our VA" bumper sticker too.

Why this book?

In my previous book, *5 Disturbing Fact About the Veterans Administration*, I outlined five facts to support my case that the current veterans' healthcare system is abusing veterans' rights. This is a volume of stories to support my arguments for change.

In the earlier book I supplied facts. The stories in this book connect the facts to real life. Now you will read about everyday veterans who have experienced the horror of bad healthcare at the Veterans Administration.

We ask our military personnel to leave their families, their friends and the comforts we enjoy in this country to serve in foreign lands, often hostile, to ensure that we can continue

ShutDownTheVA@gmail.com

to enjoy our freedoms. In recent years, this has meant multiple deployments with minimal recuperative leave time, leaving them drained of their spirits.

And what do they get when they return home, having survived conflicts of war, scarred from these harsh realities?

They get the Veterans Administration, where some go to heal, only to lose their life in a VA hospital bed. Or they are disfigured. Or in their suffering of invisible anguish that others cannot see or understand, they kill themselves.

Federal Tort Claims Act

In *5 Disturbing Facts About the Veterans Administration,* I summarized what happens when a VA doctor does something wrong during a procedure or a consultation.

The dilemma for veterans is that they cannot sue the VA like their civilian counterpart, who can take their provider to court for malpractice.

Malpractice is formally defined as "…improper, illegal, or negligent professional activity or treatment, especially by a medical practitioner, lawyer, or public official.[1]"

Malpractice can be a mistake, or it can be intentional. Typically, that's for the court to decide.

---

[1] https://www.lexico.com/en/definition/malpractice

ShutDownTheVA@gmail.com

But veterans don't get to go to court with their malpractice claims, a constitutional right guaranteed to civilian Americans. Instead, their claim must be sent to the VA Regional Counsel, a branch of the vast Veterans Administration bureaucracy. Here, the merit of the veterans' claim is judged. Do you think it will be judged fairly and impartially when the organization indicted on alleged misconduct, the VA, oversees the claim decision? Of course not.

The reason veterans cannot file a claim in a regular court of law is because their complaint is against the Veterans Administration and it's a branch of the federal government. Suing the government is restricted because of an old legal precedent called sovereign immunity, which started with kings and queens centuries ago. They were the heads of government and they were believed to be ordained by God to rule. This concept carried forward when resolving complaints against the government: The King is never wrong. We, that is, each of us as citizens, have replaced the kings and queens as the head of government in the United States. In applying the concept of sovereign immunity, which is still considered valid, this means that you, the citizen, cannot sue yourself. That is, unless you give permission.

Because of sovereign immunity, veterans were prohibited from filing any claim for damages.

After decades of outcry, Congress allowed veterans to file for damages under the Federal Tort Claims Act.

ShutDownTheVA@gmail.com

> *Under the FTCA, the federal government acts as a self-insurer, and recognizes liability for the negligent or wrongful acts or omissions of its employees acting within the scope of their official duties. The United States is liable to the same extent an individual would be in like circumstances. The statute substitutes the United States as the defendant in such a suit and the United States—not the individual employee—bears an resulting liability.[2]*

Herein lies another deficiency of the FTCA. The defendant, in most cases a doctor, never bears the responsibility for the act of malpractice.

This is the veterans only recourse for malpractice. But it is a flawed remedy because the FTCA deprives the veteran of due process, which is important to ensuring a fair hearing.

And then there's the paperwork, which the veteran handles, never knowing if it is done correctly.

Filing a FTCA using Form 95 is excruciating. The VA likes to represent the form as so easy even a third grader could file a claim. The truth is far from it. The entire system is rigged against the veteran and the process is long, complicated, and

---

[2] https://www.house.gov/doing-business-with-the-house/leases/federal-tort-claims-act

often resolves in rulings against the veteran, setting the stage for an appeal. Get the picture? Years. Years. Years. And then the veteran dies. Claim dropped. Next.

The byproduct of this awful practice is the reduction of quality care at the Veterans Administration. Employees are protected. If a claim is filed against them the Justice Department defends them. There is no way a veteran will have success with this system of justice…because it's not a system of justice at all.

VA Medical Malpractice History[3]

Investigative reporting by Diane Sawyer in 2004 is a benchmark for modern complaints about the Veterans Administration. "Primetime Thursday" revealed to the nation that a Navy Vietnam veteran named Terry Soles sought treatment at a VA hospital when he developed symptoms of intense abdominal pain and diarrhea. Mr. Soles spent two years going to the VA, without any remission of his symptoms, being told there was no real problem with his health. But his wife wasn't convinced the VA knew what they were talking about and encouraged her husband to visit a private doctor. The diagnosis this time? Cancer. But it was too late for Terry Soles, who died shortly thereafter.

Two years later, in 2006, 63 cases of malpractice at the VA were reported between 1997 to 2002. The cause? Failure of

---

[3]https://www.lawyersandsettlements.com/lawsuit/veteran_medical_malpractice.html

ShutDownTheVA@gmail.com

supervisors to properly oversee residents who were incorrectly prescribing medication, making surgical mistakes, misdiagnosing patients and giving generally unacceptable and inadequate care.

The problems continued for several years. Patients bled to death after surgery. A cancer treatment program was shuttered because the incorrect radiation doses were being given. Thousands of veterans, over a period of several years and at several VA facilities, were exposed to HIV and hepatitis when it was discovered endoscopic equipment was not being properly sterilized. A doctor was misdiagnosing patients and then given the wrong medications as treatment 56% of the time.

Despite all of these errors in patient care, administrators at these hospitals were receiving bonuses ranging from $7,000 to nearly $63,000 a year.

And what does the VA say about all of this? How do they respond to inquiries by the public? Congress? The usual response from the Veterans Administration is to refuse to release information, as they did in 2014 when direct questions were asked by the House Veterans Oversight and Investigations Hearing. They simply refused.

An organization out of control? More than that, I'm afraid. The Veterans Administration is not just an organization of bumbling fools. Unfortunately, an insidious network of career bureaucrats lines the hallways, doing everything they can to protect their jobs at the expense of veteran healthcare. These malicious individuals are destroying the credibility of

ShutDownTheVA@gmail.com

an agency also employing thousands of dedicated professionals who toil every day to help us, the nation's veterans.

My gratitude is extended to those who toil compassionately. For the others, I say "tear it down." Why? The current VA, as a cabinet level agency inside the federal government, is a good example of why government should not be running hospitals. A self-policing organization cannot be trusted. Period.

Join with me as we yank the VA out of the hands of politicians and bureaucrats and privatize it with government funding. This will restore veteran's constitutional rights and give veterans the proper oversight to ensure their care matches what is available in the civilian world.

Change come with little acts of caring. Let's turn that flag right side up. OK?

Sign me…

- A Concerned Veteran

ShutDownTheVA@gmail.com

Penile Implants

ShutDownTheVA@gmail.com

Worldwide, penile implants are a fast-growing section of business for medical device manufacturers. In 2016, the global *market* for *penile implants* was valued at around USD 232 million dollars.[4]

To be covered by insurance, including the Veterans Administration, penile implants must be prescribed for male erectile dysfunction.

These devices come in a variety of styles and each offers a different method for inflating the flaccid penis into an erection. The industry offers implants that cater to different ethnicities and each device can be customized for each penis size.

It might surprise you to know that the VA performs more of these surgeries than any other healthcare organization in the world. Don't try to confirm that. The VA will not tell you. Neither will the medical manufacturers who make and sell the devices.

That's because the VA is used for evaluating these devices on veterans as well as giving surgeons a place to practice.

The most popular implant works in a straightforward, mechanical way. First, a tube is implanted under the foreskin and along the penis shaft. This tube is attached to a pump

---

[4] https://www.prnewswire.com/news-releases/penile-implants-or-penile-prosthesis-market---global-industry-analysis-size-share-trends-and-forecast-2015--2023-300558727.html

inside the scrotum. The pump is connected to another tube that runs to a reservoir of liquid implanted above the groin in the belly. When an erection is desired, the pump in the groin is squeezed repeatedly. This causes the fluid in the reservoir to flow into the tube on the penis. Voila. Erection.

To release the erection, the pump in the scrotum is squeezed and held until the fluid flows back into the reservoir.

Penile Implants do not come without risk. For one, the healing process is not fun. But there are other unique side effects and potential complications that can arise, (no pun intended), including surgical errors.

ShutDownTheVA@gmail.com

Story #1

2012

My Story – Tubing and Horrible Surgery

I will tell my own penile implant story first.

Seven years ago, I let a resident persuade me to get the Coloplast Penile Implant.

I say "persuade" because I wasn't sold on the idea. The thought of having my groin cut open in the operating room and having someone's fingers putting in all that hardware was a big turn-off.

And his sales pitch was obviously more about giving him practice with the surgery than benefiting me.

(That's the way the VA runs. They are teaching hospitals where veterans are guinea pigs for students to practice their medical specialization.)

The resident assured me his supervisor, a licensed and experienced urology surgeon, who was very experienced at

ShutDownTheVA@gmail.com

these surgeries, would be doing the surgery and that he, the resident, would be aiding.

I said yes.

After the surgery, I was in more pain than I had ever felt in my life. I mean it was awful, awful, awful. I was on the maximum dose of morphine, but it did not help. The surgery required an overnight hospital stay. The hours dragged.

By the time I was discharged the next morning, the pain was no less excruciating. The ride home was like sitting on a giant pin cushion. Every bump in the road felt like a spear.

After the seventh day of recovery at home, I thought my groin looked as bad as the day I left the hospital. I didn't realize it could swell so much down there and not explode.

Within a month, as I recall – yes, a month - the swelling was reduced, and the pain was nearly gone. But something was wrong. My penis was crooked (it hadn't been before.) And the scrotum was larger, not from swelling, just larger.

When I returned for the follow-up appointment, I saw a different resident than the one who had talked me into the implant. He had graduated.

This new resident seemed reluctant to discuss the crooked penis and the distended scrotum. He was embarrassed when he asked me to show him the implant. He instructed me how to work the pump, but when I stumbled, he refused to aid me. Instead, he blushed.

ShutDownTheVA@gmail.com

Now I was extremely nervous. The penis was inflated, and I could not deflate it. He kept telling me what to do but I struggled. He simply would not touch me. No one should go into the urology field if you're a prude or squeamish. After 5 minutes I was able to deflate the erection. He told me there was no disfigurement, that the surgery had been successful.

After about two months, when I could feel and see the various parts of the implant in my groin, it was obvious what was wrong.

The inflation tube that was supposed to run in a straight line along the shaft of the penis was crooked. And the scrotum was full of tubing, much more than I needed.

I didn't need to be a doctor to figure any of this out. But what do I do next?

I made an appointment and met with the prudish resident again. I got major blowback from him. Another meeting with his supervisor, an attending physician in the Urology department, didn't go any better. They both said everything looked fine and didn't understand my concern.

Then I received a copy of my medical notes, including the surgical notes from the operation itself. The first resident, the one who had talked me into this developing nightmare, had signed the forms and made the notes. The doctor I believed to be the surgeon on duty signed off on nothing.

ShutDownTheVA@gmail.com

Could my worse fear be true? Had the resident done the procedure, all of it, and without anyone looking over his shoulder.

I requested another meeting with the doctor who was supposed to do the procedure, the same doctor who had been in the meeting with the prudish student. I tape recorded the meeting to protect myself.

During the meeting, he said he was in the O.R. the entire time. He contradicted written notes in my records, which I asked him about. This only made him angry.

I filed a Tort using Form 95 for the Federal Tort Claims Act. But I am not a lawyer and all the paperwork was an intimidating process, not to mention that I was complaining about a penile implant, which was also embarrassing to discuss.

So, I tried to find legal help at the VA. But there was no one to aid me. I filled out the form and sent it in. My claim for a second surgery to fix the mistakes was denied. The ruling said there was nothing wrong with the implant as given to me.

It is now 7 years since the penile implant surgery was performed. I have lived with this painful wad of excess tubing in my scrotum all that time. I can't urinate standing up because the tubing causes my penis to bend. The tubing rubs my swollen groin against my legs, chafing the skin raw and causing infections.

ShutDownTheVA@gmail.com

Three years ago, I got an appointment with a VA doctor at another facility and without knowing my history, he examined me. I said nothing, waiting for his observations. He was shocked at the poor placement of the penis tube and said I had at least an extra foot of tubing in my scrotum. He wrote this in my medical records.

Finally, I had verification of what I knew to be true. Then suddenly, when I asked for remedial surgery, this doctor was suddenly unavailable.

Finally, I was able to get an appointment at another VA facility with a different doctor. He was encouraging. He agreed the implant needed replacing and would do the surgery. Hallelujah!

Then I told him I wanted it out. No replacement, just take it out, take it out!

I'm still waiting. I do have a surgery date for January 2020. But I'm not holding my breath. The VA seems reluctant to operate because it's like an admission of guilt. I just want it gone from my body.

So I wait, fingers crossed.

Yet my problem is nothing compared to what happened to Mr. Nash. Read on.

ShutDownTheVA@gmail.com

Story #2

2012

Compiled from several sources including a story from the NY Daily News. Thank you for permission to reprint portions o the story. Thank you for taking care of veterans, those who serve to protect you. Please visit their website to say thanks. www.nydailynews.com

This is the most bizarre story I have ever heard about a botched penile implant surgery. No man deserves to have this happen. Well, maybe Jeffrey Epstein. But certainly not this man.

Frostbite

In 2012, a veteran in Kentucky made headlines. According to the New York Daily News[5], this veteran, Michael D. Nash of Louisville, Kentucky, filed suit in the U.S. District Court of Louisville alleging malpractice at a Veterans Administration Hospital in Lexington, Kentucky.

---

[5] https://www.nydailynews.com/news/national/man-sues-frostbitten-penis-article-1.1173538

Mr. Nash was asking for $10 million in damages because he had lost his penis. The cause, he claimed, was frostbite.
The New York Daily News, quoting the man's lawyer, said that Mr. Nash had served in the Army in 1968 to 1969 and required surgery on his penis and groin area.

According to the lawsuit he filed, On October 28, 2010, Mr. Nash,61, had circumcision and penile implant surgery, but afterwards, things took a turn for the worse when "… a Veterans Administration nurse repeatedly, for 19 hours solid, put ice packs on his penis after surgery, causing frostbite and gangrene and ultimately leading to the organ's partial amputation."[6]

Nash's attorney, **Larry Jones** of Jones Ward law firm in Louisville, went on to say, "It basically caused frostbite on his penis, which eventually caused gangrene. In addition to robbing someone of their manhood, they've robbed him of the simple ability to urinate just like every other person who lives in this world."[5]

Nash lost 5 inches of his penis to this incompetence and required reconstructive surgery just to be able to urinate.

As Nash's attorney went on to say, "It's about the most blatant medical malpractice error one could make," Jones said. "It's a senseless tragedy that should never have happened."

---

[6] https://www.nydailynews.com/news/national/man-sues-frostbitten-penis-article-1.1173538

ShutDownTheVA@gmail.com

Remember, Nash was at a Veterans Affairs facility, a government facility. To pursue compensation, he was required to file under the Federal Tort Claims Act. So, he did. The Department of Veterans Affairs rejected his claim, stating, "It is our opinion that there was no negligence on the part of the Department of Veterans Affairs or any of its employees in connection with the claimed loss; therefore your claim is denied," wrote Melinda Frick, Indianapolis-based regional counsel for the VA.

Mr. Nash then filed his suit in the U.S. District Court in 2012.

You can read the lawsuit that was filed by Mr. Nash. Go to:

i2.cdn.turner.com/cnn/2012/images/10/03/nash.pdf

Update?
There is no further information about this case. Mr. Nash's lawyer has not answered my email as of this writing. If anyone knows what happened to Mr. Nash, please send me an e-mail at shutdowntheva@gmail.com.

ShutDownTheVA@gmail.com

Story #3

1997

"I felt like a guinea pig" that stuck out as relevant. And note the Jackson, Mississippi VA, which will pop up again in another story.

Dicked Over [7]

This story is compiled from a series of sources. *Reprinted with permission of the the Washington City Paper. Thank you for taking care of veterans, those who serve to protect you. Please visit their website to say thanks.* *www.washingtoncitypaper.com*

By Julie Wakefeld, Aug 29, 1997 12 AM

Penile implants were sold as a safe cure for impotence, but a D.C. lawyer says the manufacturer gave his clients the shaft.

---

[7]

https://www.washingtoncitypaper.com/news/article/130137 78/dicked-over

Fred Colelli used to consider himself a regular Don Juan.

"I was very, very, very active sexually," says the 68-year-old. Active, that is, until August 1994, when he had a penile implant installed to treat a rare erectile problem. Although penile implants are generally used to treat problems of impotence, Colelli will tell you in no uncertain terms that he had had no problem sustaining erections prior to his surgery.

He opted for the implant because his penis curved at a 45-degree angle as a result of a rare affliction called Peyronie's disease. Although his organ was fully operational, the bend made his partner uncomfortable during intercourse, so he opted for surgical intervention.

What happened next sounds like a crude barroom joke. After the device was installed in the operating room, he couldn't get it to deflate. His surgeon managed to get it to go down, after a two-week waiting period, but only after a struggle. By the time Colelli got to the hospital elevator, however, it was back up again. He had to cover his obviously bulging unit with a newspaper on the bus ride home.

Colelli called the manufacturer, and a sympathetic executive there FedExed him a video on how to operate the apparatus, but Colelli still couldn't get it down and the pain became more excruciating. He says the problem became so painful he contemplated jumping off a bridge.

Colelli, who lives in Pittsburgh, went to see specialist after specialist without success. After three months of chronic pain, he had his defective implant removed—and his

ShutDownTheVA@gmail.com

manhood went with it. Nowadays, "You could hit my penis with a sledgehammer and I wouldn't feel it," he says. What's left of his surgically altered appendage is smaller than his pinkie.

His penis, he says, has "basically disappeared," but adds, "I must say I was kind of proud of what I did have."

Colelli's story might spark some smirking around the water cooler, but there's really nothing funny about it. Thirty million American men are afflicted with some form of impotence, and over 250,000 men have turned to penile implants as a fix. A sizable number of them—at least 10 percent—have found that what they had hoped was an answer to their prayers has left them with a useless device occupying some very precious real estate.

Don Bulmer wanted to cure his tendency toward brief erections, so he had an inflatable prosthesis put in at Washington Veteran's Hospital. His problem was the opposite of Colelli's: After five revision surgeries over three years, he still could not get the device to inflate. He finally had it removed.

"It may seem unbelievable what guys will go through to have sex again," Bulmer says. "But that's a big part of a man's life."

Another Washington-area man who didn't want his name used had hoped an implant installed in 1991 would fortify his flagging lily, which was ailing as a result of diabetes and a heart condition. But his device neither goes up all the

ShutDownTheVA@gmail.com

way—nor down all the way. It's a soft-on, stuck somewhere in the middle. "We still can have intercourse, but it's not what we expected it to be," he says. Both he and his wife based their expectations in part on a promotional video they viewed in the doctor's office. "Let's just say my wife told me it wasn't like what we saw in the video."

Inflatable penile implants were touted as a sure-fire cure for hard-to-treat cases of impotence. But instead of sowing marital harmony, some of the devices have been quietly wreaking havoc in bedrooms across the country. More than 25,000 device failures have been reported to the U.S. Food and Drug Administration (FDA) in Gaithersburg, Md. Many other men are likely suffering in silence.

But Colelli, Bulmer, and hundreds of other men with failed implants nationwide aren't going to take the shaft lying down; they are suing the maker of the implants for damages to their most precious asset. The plaintiffs have retained Washington attorney Lewis Saul to confront the manufacturer of their devices, American Medical Systems Inc. (AMS), a fully owned subsidiary of Pfizer. The plaintiffs allege that AMS knowingly made and marketed defective devices—and failed to warn doctors and patients of the risks. Saul may not be able to retrieve their manhood, but he's hoping to make AMS pay a pretty penny for allegedly taking it away.

"The devices have much, much lower success rates than advertised, and satisfaction rates are much lower," says Saul, who says his 300 cases make him the nation's leading attorney in penile implant litigation. Saul is waging a war on

AMS from his upper-Wisconsin Avenue office, across from Mazza Gallerie. The only thing vaguely phallic in his office is an 8-foot art-deco replica of the Statue of Liberty. He believes that when AMS put an inadequately tested product on the market, the company robbed many men of their sexual freedom.

Colelli and Bulmer aren't even Saul's toughest cases. A few of the plaintiffs have lost their penises entirely to infection. And Saul claims that the device led one man to suicide. When a penile implant goes awry, a host of other complications can arise: spontaneous inflation, erosion or migration of the implant, scar tissue buildup, chronic pain, and sensory loss. Most of these problems eventually lead to the device's removal, which leaves the man worse off than before.

"Implants should be considered irreversible," Saul says, because of damage to the natural erection system on installation. "Once you have an implant, you can't have sexual relations without an implant," Saul explains.

Saul has become the master of disaster when it comes to penile implants after years of getting weaned on litigation over altered breasts that didn't live up to expectations. Many women sued manufacturers of breast implants after the devices began leaking, sometimes sparking catastrophic infections.

He got his start in penis suits after he attended the American Trial Lawyers Association annual meeting in 1993, where he heard penile implant horror stories that pricked his

ShutDownTheVA@gmail.com

professional interest. For Saul, it was a natural transition. Breasts and penises are both sources of sexual gratification, insecurity, and no small amount of vanity. But getting your penis overhauled is a little more complicated than lifting and separating.

The penile version of an implant has movable parts that are often installed in both the testes and the shaft. To do the job, the device has to inflate on demand. And, hopefully, at some convenient point, deflate.

Problems with penile implants haven't attracted the media attention breast implants have, despite the fact that penile implants seem to be failing at very high rates.

"Society has a more difficult time talking about penises than breasts," Saul surmises. To date, Saul, who works on a contingency basis, has settled about 80 penile implant cases against manufacturers, for undisclosed sums. Saul, along with other attorneys, was able to certify the plaintiffs as a class action in a Cincinnati, Ohio, court, but AMS appealed and the class was decertified. A declaration of a class of plaintiffs would have allowed the current plaintiffs' lawyers to sue on behalf of thousands of others. Saul and his associates did manage to have the cases consolidated into a single case in Minnesota that will likely go to trial in 1998 and include the company's entire line of penile devices marketed over its past 20 years in the business. AMS dominates the market; its penis boosters have been implanted in more than 150,000 men.

Saul is also battling AMS and Pfizer close to home, spearheading a class-action fight for D.C. residents who had any surgery in a local hospital involving a Hydroflex penile prosthesis that failed. AMS began manufacturing and marketing the Hydroflex in 1985. Saul considers it "an especially faulty device" that was not replaced until the Dynaflex model debuted in 1990. Saul advertised in the Washington Post and the Washington Times to recruit local clients. Dozens of potential plaintiffs responded.

Bulmer was one of them. His Hydroflex device was first implanted at Washington Veteran's Hospital in 1979, before AMS widely marketed the product. For each of his six operations, the surgeons had to go through his lower abdomen, closing the incision with some 30-plus stitches every time.

"I think I was a guinea pig, really," says Bulmer, a 72-year-old World War II veteran who has epilepsy as a result of a B-17 bomber crash in 1942. But his penis perils made going down with the plane pale in comparison. "I deserve seven purple hearts for what I went through," he says.

AMS refuses to comment on the specifics of the pending litigation. "It's company policy that anything of a legal nature is reserved for the courtroom," says AMS spokesperson Denise Ulrich.

Saul, on the other hand, sees opportunity in talking up a problem most people aren't interested in hearing about. Product liability lawyers have a reputation as predatory creatures who feed off others' misfortune, but Saul comes

ShutDownTheVA@gmail.com

across as a mild-mannered, straightforward guy with few pretensions about his trade. And he doesn't have to stifle any Beavisesque giggles when he uses the term "penile implant." "This is just what I do for a living," he says. "They're just devices."

Law is actually a second career for the Connecticut-born Saul, who is now 48. His office showcases some of his works from his days as a painter and potter, an avocation he was forced to relegate to a hobby after he found himself with four kids and few willing buyers. Saul was barely out of George Mason University Law School when he developed an interest in product liability litigation. A friend of his became sterile after wearing a Dalkon Shield, a devilish-looking intrauterine contraceptive device. At the time, the FDA didn't require the kind of testing of contraceptive devices that other medical applications were routinely subjected to. Eventually it was discovered that the string attached to the device had a tendency to wick bacteria up into the uterus. Tens of thousands of women contracted pelvic inflammatory disease, many became sterile as a result of the device, and 18 women died. "One thing led to another, and eventually I was representing 500 clients," he says. Nearly 200,000 women filed claims against the manufacturer; they were eventually settled.

Much like the Dalkon Shield, inflatable penile implants made it to the market without extensive testing. Both were on the market before the 1976 Medical Device Amendments were made to the Food, Drug, and Cosmetic Act, which gave the FDA regulatory control over medical devices. Under the law, penile implants were essentially grandfathered: They were allowed to stay on the market with the understanding that the FDA would later require manufacturers to demonstrate their safety and effectiveness.

But the FDA has acted very slowly. Penile implants have been available since the early 1970s, and the agency didn't consider reviewing them until the spring of 1993. "I don't commend the FDA for the speed with which they've dealt with this. They still haven't published a final rule, when it should have been done 15 years ago," Saul says. Saul points out that after a similar review in 1992, silicone-gel breast implants were taken off the market.

The FDA expects to issue a final regulation in early 1998 that would require a comprehensive pre-market approval process for the devices, according to Sharon Snider, an FDA spokesperson. "We have had concerns about the numbers of complaints with these devices," she says. AMS, says Ulrich, insists it has complied with current FDA regulations for revising and changing product lines.

A stalwart phallus is the universal symbol of power. The eternally rock-hard Washington Monument provides towering visual evidence of our culture's fascination with the male member. It's no surprise, then, that impotence is unmentionable in polite company. Not only does the affliction obliterate performance in the bedroom, it eats at a man's self-confidence and sense of self-worth. "Impotence is really embarrassing. A man feels like he's not a man anymore," says Bulmer, who to this day doesn't know the cause of his particular case.

ShutDownTheVA@gmail.com

Largely due to social stigma and embarrassment, "A lot of men go untreated," says Leroy M. Nyberg Jr., director of the National Institutes of Health's (NIH's) urology programs. NIH estimates that somewhere between 10 and 30 million American men suffer from impotence, which is defined as a consistent inability to sustain an erection sufficient for sexual intercourse. Although impotence is not an inevitable part of aging, its incidence rises with age. By age 65, about 20 percent of men have experienced impotence.

The inability to rise on cue is usually caused by an underlying physical condition, such as kidney disease, multiple sclerosis, or circulatory abnormalities like arteriosclerosis or vascular disease. Up to 50 percent of men with diabetes, for instance, experience impotence. Surgery or injury to the prostate, bladder, pelvis, or rectum can damage key nerves and tissues involved in erections and lead to impotence. Many drugs, including blood pressure medications, anti-depressants, ulcer drugs, tranquilizers, and street drugs, often produce impotence as a side effect. Alcohol and nicotine can also be problematic. Psychological factors are estimated to be the primary cause of only about 10 to 20 percent of impotence cases. Ultimately, Nyberg says, "We don't know the real underlying cause."

A hard-on may seem like a simple enough affair but getting it up requires complex interplay between brain stimuli, nerve impulses, blood vessel function, and hormone levels, a ballet of physiology that still baffles researchers. Even if they lack an underlying understanding of its causes, scientists have managed to produce new and better treatments over the past three decades. Penile implants are not the treatment of choice for garden-variety impotence. A guy has to be in serious distress to allow anyone to cut his penis, let alone insert complicated machinery into it. Not surprisingly, as failure rates have become more broadly known in the medical community, the use of penile implants is declining. "They are being used less frequently these days," Nyberg says. "The trend is toward nonoperative management of impotence." Drugs can have profound effects in some patients, while others use exterior mechanical devices such as vacuums to get their penises to stand at attention.

While popping a pill to get erect works for some men, the available drugs are not always effective. Creams sometimes work to help sustain an erection, but the leading alternative is to take a syringe and inject drugs like asprostadil and papaverine hydrochloride to restore potency by dilating blood vessels. Asprostadil can also be administered in a suppository form. The downside is obvious—once the bearer has used his erect penis for the only thing it's good for, he wants it to return to its naturally flaccid state. Injections and creams can cause prolonged erections, which can be painful and cause scarring of penile tissue.

Some 100,000 otherwise limp penises rely on external vacuum devices to get hard by drawing blood into the penis. The cylindrical apparatus is used in tandem with a constriction band to maintain the erection for up to a half-hour. Vascular surgery to repair restricted arteries or leaky blood vessels in the penis also helps some men.

The alternatives have not advanced enough to render inflatable implants obsolete, however. "There will always be

ShutDownTheVA@gmail.com

a place for penile implants in the man who doesn't respond to drugs," Nyberg says. Though the latest injections are effective in 80 to 90 percent of men, more than 25,000 still choose implants every year. For some, the one-time trauma of having a device implanted beats the alternative. "There was no way I was going to stick a needle in my penis every time I wanted to do it. I already was injecting myself in the arm every day for diabetes," says one District implant user. The goal of obtaining sustainable erections in impotent men has received a fair amount of effort over the years. Surgeons began experimenting in the 1930s with methods to produce artificial erections. The first prosthesis was actually a rib graft, which led to the implantation of the first synthetic material in the penis in 1950. In the wake of the Vietnam War, research was stepped up to assist American soldiers coming home maimed and mutilated.

When they work, modern-day inflatable penile implants represent an engineering minimarvel. Fully pumped, as Hans and Franz would say, the devices have the same internal pressure as that of an automobile tire—about 30 pounds per square inch. And during sexual congress, the devices—which are made of silicone rubber or polyurethane rubber—undergo additional external pressure. The wear and tear is obviously substantial.

"The technology has advanced phenomenally—having learned a lot from early failures," says Nyberg. "It's a very difficult device to make."

The inflatable or hydraulic implants, which run from $10,000 to $15,000 including installation, typically consist

ShutDownTheVA@gmail.com

of three parts: a twin set of inflatable cylinders inserted into the shaft of the penis, a pump placed in the scrotum, and a reservoir of saline solution stowed under the abdominal muscles. The entire apparatus is implanted through a small incision at the base of the penis, where it joins the scrotum. Once in place, the rubbery device theoretically provides erections on demand. The user rapidly squeezes the pump nestled in his balls, forcing fluid from the reservoir into the shaft and expanding the twin cylinders.

The man can stay firmly inflated for as long as he or his partner desires, and if things are working right, he can even come—many implant wearers have the capacity for ejaculation if no nerve injury has occurred during implantation. In theory, the pump is simply squeezed again to deflate.

Other hydraulic models have two parts and suspend the reservoir in the scrotum. Still others house all the components within the penis itself and inflate when the tip of the penis is massaged. There are also nonhydraulic semirigid and malleable implants that consist of permanently stiff rods that can be folded out of the way when not in use. The noninflatable devices involve less risk because they have no moving parts but are more unsightly and can cause embarrassment in locker rooms and the like, as the man essentially has a perma-hard-on.

Unlike silicone counterparts installed in women's breasts, penile implants usually diminish in size over time. Even with inflatables, the erection is generally smaller: about an inch or two shorter in length than a natural one, along with a

ShutDownTheVA@gmail.com

diminished circumference. The erection is also less rigid than a natural hard-on, and the head of the penis is softer, according to Bernie Zilbergeld, author of The New Male Sexuality. "An implant will change only the stiffness of your penis, not your personality, behavior, or lovemaking technique," Zilbergeld writes. "And it most certainly will not save a failing relationship."

Although both of the inflatable AMS devices implanted in Don Bulmer eventually failed, one of the devices worked for a year or so, and during that time he was pleased with the erection it generated. "It was just about natural," he says. "When you lose everything and [then] can actually do it, it's unreal."

Attorney Saul has nothing against restoring men's sexual prowess. "The concept of helping men achieve erection is a good concept if it can be done in a moral and effective way," Saul says. Saul charges that AMS, "a company that's selling hope," was negligent in development of the devices and failed to adequately inform his clients of the risks associated with them.

F. Brantley Scott, who co-founded AMS in 1972 and is one of the pioneers of the inflatable penile implant, hawked his inflatable wares on the Phil Donahue show in July 1979. Scott told the audience that he got interested in implants while treating paraplegics during his days as a physician in a veterans hospital. He went on to become the head of the urology department at Baylor College of Medicine in Houston. On the show, he claimed that the inflatable devices produced an erection "indistinguishable from a normal

ShutDownTheVA@gmail.com

erection." At the time, Scott was still a partner in AMS, which was bought out by the corporate Goliath Pfizer in 1985.

In response to an audience question about how long the devices would last, Scott downplayed the risks: "Unfortunately, we really don't know. We'll know a lifetime from now whether or not it will last a lifetime. Some of the bench testing with silicone rubber, which is a very inert material, would indicate that at least probably the majority of the implants will last the lifetime of the patient. Fortunately, however, if there is a problem, it's usually relatively minor surgery to make a correction, and we've done that."

Today, AMS claims it has never made any guarantees about the life expectancy, success, or satisfaction rates of its devices. In addition, the company says, data on revision and replacements has been easy to access. "The information has always been readily available in the literature to any physician working with the product," says AMS's Ulrich. Between the lines, AMS likes to imply that if there is a problem with the machine, it probably has something to do with the person who installed it. "Each surgeon has a different success rate with this, as well as with any other surgical procedure," Ulrich says.

Saul charges that AMS has been less than forthcoming with actual failure rates. "Many of the doctors are not told the full truth. The medical community is being misled," Saul says. For starters, AMS was cited several times in the late '80s for failing to report device failures and revision surgeries to the

ShutDownTheVA@gmail.com

FDA, and it has never released long-term follow-up data on the devices.

The body of medical literature on penile implants is incomplete and difficult to interpret, in part because the devices are constantly under revision. New models are introduced before the medical community gets a handle on the efficacy rates of the ones currently in use. Saul says that in depositions doctors across the board say they're not aware of the failure rates. "How's the doctor supposed to be aware? They only know by clinical experience," he says. "And how are the patients supposed to know if the doctors don't know?" Saul asks.

It wasn't until 1993 that AMS put out a pamphlet formally disclosing overall revision rates of its latest inflatable devices. The information has also been available on its web page since May of this year. For the AMS 700 CX, a three-part device, the company reports a revision and replacement rate of 8 percent within the first five years. For the AMS 700 Ultrex, another three-parter, the rate is 10 percent within two years. And for the Dynaflex, which is a hydraulic device contained within the penis and activated by tip massage, it reports a 9 percent rate within three years. In the fine print, the company acknowledges that these are only average failure rates and that they do not include devices that had not yet been removed at the time of the study. "The reality is they are mechanical devices," Ulrich says, the implication being that even the best machines occasionally succumb to stress.

ShutDownTheVA@gmail.com

Colelli, like hundreds of other patients who are part of Saul's national case, claims he was never properly warned of the real risks. "They never told me I would be impotent," says Colelli. "I wasn't informed about the outcome. I was told of the positive outcomes only."

Men who are living with impotence tend to trust what they are being told. "I was told that the device was the best one on the market at the time," says one Washingtonian whose implant is stuck in limp limbo.

Saul charges that AMS used men in its target market as guinea pigs. "AMS engaged in human engineering instead of investing in research and development," Saul says. "These devices are all bound to fail at some point."

"When the devices first came into being, [the failure rates] were very high," agrees NIH's Nyberg. "But you have to look at it as when the failures occurred." Technology has since improved, Nyberg says, and "the devices have a high mechanical success rate. Whether the patient or partner satisfaction is as high is hard to tell." Unprompted, Nyberg adds that he personally has no experience with or need for an implant.

The devices may be working much better today, Saul acknowledges, but "the technology clearly wasn't there when they started marketing [them]." And in fact, Saul has some clients with failed devices implanted within the last year.

The National Library of Medicine in Bethesda in a 1990 video details the one- to three-hour implant surgery. Penile

ShutDownTheVA@gmail.com

pioneer Scott, who by then had left AMS and is now deceased, appears on the tape. "Restoring quality of life in the bedroom has been a satisfying experience for the surgeon, the patient, and his wife," he says. "Try it; you'll like it."

ShutDownTheVA@gmail.com

Story #4

2005

This story is told in a different format. It is a ruling from the Veterans Appeal Board, and this is what a veteran receives when the board decides the outcome of an appeal.

The judges do an excellent job of being bureaucratic, impersonal, and deflecting blame away from the VA. And once you're finished, I am sure you'll understand why veterans are so frustrated with their treatment.

The veterans name is redacted. The decision is printed verbatim.

From the Files of the Veterans Appeal Board
Citation Nr: 0509221 [8]

Decision Date: 03/28/05   Archive Date: 04/07/05
DOCKET NO. 98-16 517
On appeal from the
Department of Veterans Affairs Regional Office in Jackson,

---

[8] https://www.va.gov/vetapp05/files2/0509221.txt

Mississippi

THE ISSUE
Entitlement to benefits under the provisions of 38 U.S.C.A. § 1151 for erectile dysfunction as a consequence of surgical treatment at a VA medical facility on July 2, 1996.

REPRESENTATION
Veteran represented by: Veterans of Foreign Wars of the United States
WITNESS AT HEARING ON APPEAL
The veteran
ATTORNEY FOR THE BOARD
A. Jaeger, Associate Counsel
INTRODUCTION
The veteran served on active duty from February 1971 to February 1974 with approximately 10 months of prior active service.

This matter comes before the Board of Veterans' Appeals (Board) on appeal from a rating decision of January 1998 from the Department of Veterans Affairs (VA) Regional Office (RO) in Jackson, Mississippi. The Board remanded this issue most recently in September 2004 for issuance of a supplemental statement of the case. The case now returns to the Board for appellate review.

FINDINGS OF FACT
1. The medical evidence of record establishes that the veteran suffered erectile dysfunction with inability to achieve or maintain an erection sufficient to have intercourse

ShutDownTheVA@gmail.com

for a period of approximately one year prior to the penile prosthesis implant performed on July 2, 1996.

2. The veteran underwent a penile prosthesis implant procedure at the Jackson VA Medical Center on July 2, 1996, following which he developed an infection requiring that the components of the prosthesis be removed, resulting in erectile dysfunction with inability to achieve or maintain an erection sufficient to have intercourse.

3. The medical evidence of record does not establish the clinical presence of additional disability as a result of the surgical procedure at a VA medical facility on July 2, 1996.

CONCLUSION OF LAW

Entitlement to benefits under the provisions of 38 U.S.C.A. § 1151 for erectile dysfunction as a consequence of surgical treatment at a VA medical facility on July 2, 1996, is not established. 38 U.S.C.A. § 1151 (West 1991); 38 C.F.R. § 3.358 (1997).

REASONS AND BASES FOR FINDINGS AND CONCLUSION

Background
The veteran served on active duty from February 1971 to February 1974 with approximately 10 months of prior active service in the United States Army.

An October 1993 outpatient treatment record from the Jackson VA Medical Center reveals that the veteran complained of lower back pain since 1971, but denied bowel,

ShutDownTheVA@gmail.com

bladder, or sexual dysfunction. VA outpatient treatment records, dated in February 1995, show that the veteran complained of neck and back pain, stating that increasing pain made it difficult to have sex.

In March 1995 the veteran was referred to the Psychology Clinic by the Genitourinary (GU) Clinic for complaints of organic impotence. In June 1995, the Sexual Dysfunction Clinic evaluated the veteran. He reported a gradual onset of decreased ability to obtain and maintain an erection sufficient for intercourse for about one year. He further related that that he was able to obtain erections sufficient for intercourse roughly 30 percent of the time during the last year, but denied morning or nocturnal erections during the past year. The veteran also indicated unsatisfactory ejaculatory control and decreased penile sensation. However, despite such sexual difficulties, he reported a fairly active sexual lifestyle, engaging in regular sexual activity and intercourse before separation from his partner two months previously, denying problems with sexual desires or pain during sexual activities, and indicating that he was not currently sexually active with any partner.

The reporting physician, the Chief of the Psychology Service, stated that laboratory tests showed that serum levels of prolactin and testosterone were within normal limits. It was noted that, although the veteran claimed that his sexual difficulties did not lead to the termination of his previous intimate relationships, he reported that his former partners complained about his sexual performance, which had led to argument, frustration and anxiety to perform. He also denied relationship problems during the onset of his sexual

ShutDownTheVA@gmail.com

dysfunction and claimed that he was able to satisfy his partners through other sexual activities. He expressed strong dissatisfaction toward his sexual functioning and expressed increased concerns toward establishing future intimate relationships due to his current sexual problems. The examining VA psychologist stated that the veteran was currently experiencing erectile dysfunction and premature ejaculation in the presence of a medication treatment regimen. The examiner also indicated that the veteran reported concerns and frustration with his current sexual functioning; however, the role of psychological factors in the exacerbation and onset of his sexual problems seemed unremarkable. It was also indicated that a thorough medical evaluation was needed to assess the biological basis for the dysfunction. It was noted by the examiner that a measure of sexual information and beliefs indicated that the veteran had a limited understanding of sexual functioning.

The reporting physician further stated that the veteran appeared to be an appropriate candidate for non-invasive treatment at this time and it was strongly recommended that a penile implant not be considered until non-invasive intervention has been proven unsuccessful and a biological basis for the sexual dysfunction had been demonstrated. It was recommended that additional medical evaluations should evaluate common organic causes of erectile dysfunction.

A VA outpatient treatment record, dated in July 1995, shows that the veteran was seen in the GU clinic for erectile dysfunction and was approved by the Psychology Clinic for

ShutDownTheVA@gmail.com

non-invasive treatment. His testosterone level was within normal limits.

A January 1996 treatment record from the GU Clinic reflects that the veteran was being followed for erectile dysfunction. He related that he had bought a vacuum device and had pain with the use of such device. The veteran described having had a blood knot with use. He indicated his interest in an implant. The reporting physician stated that he discussed an penile implant penile prosthetic (IPP) and a SRPP with the veteran. He further noted that the veteran had sent for literature on a penile prosthesis implant on his own, noting that the claimant had a history of neck and low back injuries, as well as an injury to his groin. The assessment was erectile dysfunction - failed Yocon pills, pain and hematoma with vacuum device, and no hormone studies. The veteran was referred to the psychology section for evaluation for a possible penile implant.

VA outpatient treatment records from the Sexual Dysfunction Consultation Clinic, at the Jackson VA Medical Center, dated in February 1996, show that the veteran was referred by the GU clinic for presenting complaints of erectile dysfunction for approximately 10 years, stating that this condition has gradually worsened, particularly in the past few years, and that currently he is unable to attain a firm erection (including nocturnal erections) despite intact sexual desire. He also reported premature ejaculation on most occasions. It was noted that the veteran had been treated with Yocon pills and a vacuum tumescence pump, but he was not satisfied with the results of either treatment, and, at present time, he was interested in a surgical implant device. A

ShutDownTheVA@gmail.com

review of the veteran's medical history and an interview disclosed that no etiological cause for his erectile dysfunction has been determined, but he asserted that he had been told that it is related to his back injury. The veteran underwent a mental status examination that revealed mild to moderate depression, but no significant anxiety. The veteran reported that he had never been married; that he had had a number of girlfriends, but had been unable to maintain a relationship due to his sexual dysfunction. The diagnoses were sexual dysfunction, not otherwise stated; and premature ejaculation. The physician indicated that there were no clear etiological factors had been identified for the veteran and the lack of nocturnal erection suggested probable organic involvement. It was also noted that non-invasive treatments to date had reportedly not proven effective and that the veteran was currently seeking a surgical implant. The veteran appeared to be an acceptable candidate for a surgical implant device for treatment of his erectile dysfunction and it was noted that it was important to ensure that he had realistic expectations regarding the effects of the surgery on both erectile and orgasmic function. It was recorded that the veteran was provided education regarding maintaining factors of sexual dysfunction (e.g., alcohol, marijuana, performance anxiety, relationship problems, sexual misinformation).

A June 1996 VA treatment record reflects that the veteran was being followed for erectile dysfunction for one year and had been cleared by psychology for a penile implant. Ten days later, the veteran was presented to the Impotence Board and cleared for a penile prosthesis implant.

ShutDownTheVA@gmail.com

On July 1, 1996, the veteran signed a Request for Administration of Anesthesia and For Performance of Operations and other Procedures (Standard Form 522) in which he affirmatively indicated that the nature and purpose of the operation or procedure, the possible alternative methods of treatment, the risks involved, and the possibility of complications have been fully explained to him. He also indicated that he acknowledged that no guarantees had been made to him concerning the results of the operation or procedure and that he understood the nature of the operation or procedure to be "place an inflatable penile prosthesis and/or any other indicated procedure," to be performed by or under the direction of a named surgeon and others. The counseling physician affirmed that he had counseled the veteran as to the nature of the proposed procedure(s), the attendant risks involved, and the expected results. The physician specified that the risks included death; infection; bleeding; erosion; removal of prosthesis; penile, urethral, and bladder damage; and penile shortening. The veteran affixed his signature under a statement that he understood the nature of the proposed procedure(s), the attendant risks involved, and the expected results, as described above, and hereby requested that such procedure be performed. A medical record titled Preoperative Evaluation Sheet & Informed Consent, also dated July 1, 1996, reflected that the relative aspects of the procedure/treatment, indications, risk benefits, and alternatives have been discussed with the veteran in language understandable to him. Such also indicated that the veteran freely signed the consent without duress or coercion.

ShutDownTheVA@gmail.com

A VA hospital summary from the Jackson VA Medical Center, dated from July 1 to July 4, 1996, shows that the veteran had probable organic impotence times 5 years and that he had failed treatment with Yocon and VED (vacuum erection device). It was also noted that the veteran's hormonal studies were normal and that he currently obtains very weak and infrequent partial erections that are inadequate for intercourse. It was documented that the psychiatry unit had cleared the veteran for surgery and that he had been presented to the impotence board and approved for an operation. It was noted that the veteran desired an inflatable penile prosthesis.

Following admission, the veteran underwent preoperative examination by the urology service, a Foley catheter was placed under sterile conditions, and routine lab works showed testosterone of 3.4 and prolactin of 10.8, both within normal limits. Preoperative education was completed, including post-operative expectations, including pain, intravenous medications, drainage tubes, and exercises. The veteran was subsequently taken to the operation room where, following administration of preoperative intravenous antibiotics, he underwent inflatable penile prosthesis without immediate complications. The operative report shows that copious antibiotic irrigation was utilized throughout the procedure. Following placement, the pump was cycled, resulting in an excellent, straight, rigid erection, then deflated. The veteran tolerated the procedure well, and was extubated in the recovery room and transferred in good condition. The operative notes show that there were no complications.

ShutDownTheVA@gmail.com

Hospital treatment notes show that on the first postoperative day, the veteran was afebrile, his vital signs were stable, and he was complaining of some appropriate penile swelling and pain, but was otherwise doing well. On July 3, 1996, the veteran was alert and oriented, voiced no complaints of pain or discomfort, and tolerated cleaning and diet, and medication for pain was provided. A urine sample collected on July 1, 1996, with the results dated July 3, 1996, was negative, showing no growth. He was reported to be resting quietly and in no distress. The veteran's wound was clean, dry, and intact, and he was determined to be ready for discharge to home. The discharge medications were Cipro and Keflex, and he was given pain medication and instructed to shower after three days, but not to tub bathe prior to returning to the clinic in one week. At the time of hospital discharge on July 4, 1994, nurse's notes show that the veteran was alert, oriented, and stable; in no pain, with regular bowel and bladder habits, and he voiced understanding of self care and medications, and he executed a document affirming such.

The claimant was again seen in the GU clinic on July 12, 1996, at which time he complained of pain since surgery, gradually improving. It was noted that he had no difficulty voiding, and was currently on Keflex. Examination showed that the wound was healing well, and the pump was noted to be in the dependent part of the scrotum. The assessment was penile prosthesis implant, doing well, and he was asked to return in three weeks for cycling of the prosthesis.

The veteran was seen on August 5, 1996, in the GU clinic and was noted to be status post penile prosthesis implant

ShutDownTheVA@gmail.com

with no complaints. His wound was shown to be healing well, with a very small amount of exudates at the suture line, but no purulence. The prosthesis was pumped to less than full erection. The assessment was status post penile prosthesis implant, and he was asked to return to the clinic in two weeks.

VA outpatient treatment records from the Jackson VA Medical Center show that after his follow-up appointments cited above, the veteran failed to report for scheduled appointments in the GU clinic on August 19, 1996; on December 12, 1996; and on February 28, 1997.

A hospital summary and treatment notes from Forrest General Hospital, a private medical facility, dated from August 15 to 19, 1996, show that the veteran presented at the Emergency Room on August 15, 1996, complaining of a 48-hour history of swelling and pain in the right hemiscrotum. Examination revealed severe induration of the entire scrotum with moderate swelling of the right hemiscrotum and it was noted to be exquisitely painful to examine. The impression on admission was infection of the pump device for the penile prosthesis, with probable epididymitis. The reporting physician discussed the options of attempted antibiotic salvage, but the veteran indicated that he was not interested in that mode of therapy and requested removal of the prosthesis. After a lengthy discussion, the veteran agreed to the removal of only those portions of the prosthesis which are non-functioning or infected, leaving, if possible, the corporal body prosthesis and reservoir and removing only the pump. The reporting physician noted that the shaft of the penis appeared not to be involved, the abdomen was soft and

ShutDownTheVA@gmail.com

nontender, and there was no evidence of infection around the reservoir. The veteran was then admitted to the hospital for intravenous antibiotics and taken to the operating room, where he underwent scrotal exploration and drainage of an abcess cavitity around the inflatable prosthesis pump. Intraoperative cultures revealed staph aureus. The pump capsule had ruptured on the right side, the testicle was not involved, and the pump was removed. The rods in the corporal body, reservoir, and abdominal cavity were left in place after being capped. The wound was irrigated with antibiotic-based normal saline. The veteran spiked a fever of 103 on the first postoperative day, after which he was afebrile for the remainder of his hospital course. He underwent twice daily dressing changes as the scrotal wound was left open and packed with saline moistened gauze. The sensitivities returned on the staph aureus was basically sensitive to all antibiotics tested, and he was placed on Ciprofloxin at discharge. His condition at discharge was stable and afebrile for 48 hours. The reporting physician stated that he contacted the Jackson VA Medical Center, on Friday, August 16, 1996, and discussed the veteran with one of the residents, and decided to keep the veteran and treat him with antibiotics. The veteran was noted to have an appointment that morning with the VA, and the reporting physician recommended that he keep that appointment for possible future repairs as well as assistance with obtaining antibiotics and supplies for wound care, noting the veteran's statement that he would not be able to afford any of those antibiotics or supplies.

VA outpatient treatment records from the New Orleans VA

ShutDownTheVA@gmail.com

Medical Center, dated August 22, 1996, show that the veteran was seen on that date, with the notation that a scrotal implant was removed the previous Thursday and that the veteran had an infection and was out of medications. He was noted, by history, to have undergone a penile implant at the Jackson VA Medical Center which became infected, went to a private hospital where they removed the pump and gave him prescriptions for antibiotics, which he could not afford to have filled, and he took the antibiotics for only three days. Examination disclosed an incision in his scrotum that was packed with gauze. The packing was removed, without evidence of drainage. The impression was infected penile prosthesis, status post removal prosthesis, and the veteran was given Keflex, instructed to continue dressing changes with dry gauze, and told that packing was not necessary. On August 30, 1996, the veteran was noted to be there for follow-up of an infection of a penile prosthesis, status post removal of the pump. The wound in the scrotum appeared to be healing slowly, with no drainage noted, and the plan was to continue dressing changes. The veteran was to return to the clinic in two weeks and was referred to the GU clinic. The veteran failed to report for further scheduled appointments.

A VA hospital summary and treatment notes from the Biloxi VA Medical Center, dated from September 5 to September 23, 1996, shows that the veteran was admitted for treatment of a suspected infection of his penile prosthesis and he was noted to be status pot penile prosthesis implant at the Jackson VA Medical Center on July 2, 1996. He related that in approximately the first week of August, he returned to the Jackson VA Medical Center with "infection" and was told

ShutDownTheVA@gmail.com

that "no treatment was needed; there was nothing wrong." Three days later, he was evaluated at Forrest General Hospital for the same signs and symptoms, and subsequently underwent removal on the prosthetic pump and treatment with antibiotics for "infection" as an outpatient, being discharged on August 19, 1996. He continued to have persistent genital pain and subsequently was evaluated in the Primary Care Clinic at the New Orleans VA Medical Center where he was given oral antibiotic therapy and referred for GU evaluation, scheduled for October 23, 1996. At the time of the evaluation at the Biloxi VA Medical Center, the veteran was on no antibiotic therapy and denied any improvement, stating that he "is getting worse." However, he also stated that his genitalia "looks the same as it did in early August," when he was seen at the Jackson VA Medical Center. The etiology of the erectile dysfunction was unknown to the veteran and he stated that he used the vacuum erection device approximately 11/2 to 2 years with satisfactory results except for intermittent puposal edema. It was noted that the veteran subsequently underwent penile prosthesis implantation. X-rays on the day of admission revealed penile prostheses were seen to be in place and there were no air-fluid levels seen in the scrotum or penis. The make and model of the prosthesis was unknown to the veteran and he desired treatment including removal of the penile prosthesis if necessary. Examination disclosed a very tender penis and scrotum, without erythema or induration, and a granulating scrotal incision in the midline, without evidence of mass or abcess.

The veteran was admitted to the Biloxi VA Medical Center on September 5, 1996, with the diagnosis of infected penile

ShutDownTheVA@gmail.com

prosthesis and was placed on intravenous Vancomycin. His symptoms slightly improved with that treatment, but failed to resolve. An X-ray of the pelvis revealed a penile implant and no unusual diagnostic pattern. A ultrasound of the pelvis reflected small reactive hydroceles without focal fluid collection associated with penile prosthesis. On September 11, 1996, the veteran was evaluated by mental health services and found to be suffering from severe depression and signs of suicidal ideation. He was felt to be experiencing adjustment disorder with overlying depression and anger in an appropriate response to his infected penile prosthesis as well as underlying depression for some number of years prior to admission. It was noted that he responded well to interventions and his affect improved. On September 17, 1996, the veteran's infected penile prosthesis was removed. The Operation Report revealed findings of infected penile prosthesis with specimens; left crural implant, right crural implant, and prosthetic reservoir; nectrotic material debrided from scrotal wound; and cultures of purulent material. A Surgical Pathology Report reflected a diagnosis of foreign objects, designated "infected penile prosthesis," and removal of surgical hardware compatible with penile prosthesis. He tolerated the procedure well and was discharged on postoperative day #6, tolerating a regular diet and having all his drains removed. He remained afebrile, voiding spontaneously, and ambulating without assistance. The veteran was instructed on postoperative wound care to include monitoring for signs or infection such as swelling, pain, and discharge from the wound site, and to follow-up in the GU clinic if any of those symptoms appeared. The diagnosis on hospital discharge was infected penile prosthesis.

ShutDownTheVA@gmail.com

VA outpatient treatment records from the Biloxi VA Medical Center show that the veteran was seen for follow-up on September 30, 1996, and was noted to be status post removal of an infected penile prosthesis on September 17, 1996. He was doing well, although some tenderness of the right testis was noted, and his surgical wounds were healing nicely. The veteran complained of anger, depression, insomnia, nightmares, intrusive thoughts and homicidal ideation, feeling that he will hurt someone because of his problems associated with his war injury. He was placed on Prozac and Tranzadone. Records dated in February 1997 show that the veteran experienced complete impotence, although his external genitalia were normal. The impression was erectile dysfunction, and he was given instructions in the use of the VED. In April 1997, the veteran complained that the VED "didn't work" and that he could not maintain an erection. The use of Muse was discussed, and the veteran was told that it probably would not work because of the prior penile prosthesis implant, but he wanted to try. The use of Muse produced a very minimal erection. The impression was erectile dysfunction and depression. Further instruction in the use of the VED was provided.

VA outpatient treatment records from the Biloxi VA Medical Center show that, in April 1997, the veteran reported that the Prozac was not helpful, and that Tranzadone did not help his insomnia. The veteran stated that the VA had "butchered him." The diagnoses were Axis I: dysthymia, alcohol dependence, cannabis abuse, rule out dependence, and, Axis II: antisocial personality disorder. Laboratory reports showed testosterone of 290, and prolactin

ShutDownTheVA@gmail.com

of 8.4. The veteran achieved a 50 percent erection using Muse. In May 1997, the veteran was provided Muse in 500 mg. capsules, with approximately 10 percent tumescense. The impression was erectile dysfunction, and Muse was ordered in 1000 mg. tablets.

In May 1997, a VA psychologist noted that the veteran developed erectile dysfunction likely secondary to back problems. It was also observed that he tried a VED, which did not work and that he had an implant at the Jackson VA Medical Center, which caused recurrent pain and infections. As such, it was noted that the pump was removed and, currently, that he is having marked adjustment disorders with the lack of erection ability. The impression was erectile dysfunction, post-traumatic stress disorder (PTSD), personality disorder, and, subsequently, dysthymia. In June 1997, the claimant was noted to be self-administering Muse, 1000 mg., with minimal response. The impression was erectile dysfunction, probably psychologic. Also in June 1997, he was noted to be somewhat improved, sleeping better, and denied suicidal or homicidal ideation, psychotic symptoms, or medication side effects. The impression was dysthymia.

The record shows that at a VA examination for PTSD, conducted in July 1997, the veteran asserted that his sex life has been unsatisfactory since the VA performed surgery on him "that he didn't need," that the VA used him "as a guinea pig," and lied to him. It was noted that the veteran had a great deal of anger directed toward the Urology service at the Jackson VA Medical Center. It was observed that he insisted

ShutDownTheVA@gmail.com

that he was made to undergo surgery that was not necessary, a penile implant done in July 1996 was useless, caused him to be completely impotent, and he had been unable to have intercourse for at least 11/2 years.

A report of VA genitourinary examination, conducted in December 1997, cited the examiner's review of the claims folder. The examiner also noted a history provided by the veteran of having developed erectile dysfunction approximately 10 years previously, which was thought to be organic in nature, although no actual cause had been documented. The examiner took note of the previously described history. At the time of the December 1997 VA examination, the veteran indicated no pain at the site of his surgery, but claimed a complete inability to get an erection. He specifically denied nocturnal erections. The veteran was adamant that he was lied to about the inflatable prosthesis at the Jackson VA Medical Center and felt that he was treated as a "guinea pig." In addition, the veteran stated that, subsequent to implantation of the prosthesis, when he developed an infection he was seen at the Jackson VA Medical Center and was told there was no infection. However, shortly thereafter, he was admitted to the Forrest General Hospital for treatment of an infection. The veteran stated that he felt nothing but hatred for the physicians at the Jackson VA Medical Center, that he can no longer have sex, and "his life is ruined." The impression was erectile dysfunction, original etiology unknown, and the VA examiner stated that such was probably permanent due to the implantation of a penile prosthesis, which subsequently failed and was surgically removed.

ShutDownTheVA@gmail.com

Medical records, dated in November 1998, from Dr. D.C.S, a physician at Forrest General Hospital, indicate that he had seen the veteran about one year previously when he came to the office with an infected pump to his inflatable penile prosthesis. Dr. D. indicated that he had removed the pump, but left the cylinders and reservoir in place. Dr. D. noted that the prosthesis had been placed at VA and it was an AMS device and that the veteran was very disappointed with the device. The record reflects that after the veteran was over the infection, he went down to the Gulf Coast about a month later and contracted another infection. A physician there removed the cylinders.

Dr. D. further noted that the veteran returned two weeks ago for continued problems with erectile dysfunction. A Doppler study done in November 1998 revealed that the veteran had good arterial in flow to the penis, despite the scarring of the previous inflatable prosthesis, but he had venous leak. The resistive indices were 89 on the right and 83 on the left, indicative of venogenic impotence. The veteran's peak velocities for arterial in flow were 69 on the right and 63 on the left, which Dr. D. noted to be pretty good, especially considering that the veteran had a previous prosthesis.

A personal hearing was held in February 1999 before an RO Hearing Officer. The veteran testified that he was entitled to benefits under the provisions of 38 U.S.C.A. § 1151 for erectile dysfunction as a consequence of a failed penile prosthesis at a VA medical facility on July 2, 1996. He further testified that prior to the surgery, he was having problems achieving or maintaining an erection and was not having erections during sleep as far as he knew. The veteran

ShutDownTheVA@gmail.com

stated that he first went to the Jackson VA Medical Center to talk to doctors about his foreskin swelling and was referred to the GU clinic where he was not examined, but just prescribed pills. He indicated that such pills had no effect and, as such, he returned to the GU clinic. Upon his return, he was told about the "pump"[a vacuum erection device, or VED], the doctor sent him down to the prosthesis department and the lady there refused to give him one because she stated that he had hit a deer on his motorcycle, went off the road and hit a tree with his knee; and that such was the cause of his problem with erectile dysfunction. He further testified that he returned to the doctor and told him that the lady had refused to give him a pump and that the doctor stated that he would check around to find one

The veteran testified that he then called a number in a magazine, and was given the address of a drugstore in Waynesboro, Mississippi, he went to that location and was told that the individual there could not sell him one [a VED] without some kind of written permission because they were not an over-the-counter item. The veteran stated that he returned to the Jackson VA Medical Center and obtained a prescription for the VED from the VA physician. He thereafter bought one, took it home, read the booklet, and watched the tape, and that the VED worked "great," except that it caused the foreskin on his penis to swell up and cause some discomfort for a day or two after use. He testified that he continued to have such problem when he used the VED, but it was still working great. The veteran stated that the doctor told him that he could fix that by using an implant and that it was a simple procedure that they did all the time. The veteran related that these events occurred prior to July 1996.

ShutDownTheVA@gmail.com

The veteran also testified that he was told that there would be no noticeable change in size or length and that the head of his penis would not swell up. He related that he returned on July 2, 1996, to undergo preoperative preparation. At such time he was given papers to sign. The veteran testified that he started to read the papers and was interrupted by a lady doctor who came in and started talking to his doctor. He was asked if he had read the document and he said "no" and as a response, he was told that all he needed to do was sign on the bottom. The veteran related that he told the doctor that he needed to take the document to his room to read it and was told "no, this is to ensure that your vehicle in the parking lot won't be towed or fooled with while [he] was staying there," it guarantees a lock for his room and everything and for [his] meals, and that the veteran had to trust him because he was his doctor. The veteran testified that he was further told by the doctor that if he wanted a second opinion and had the money, he could go and get one and that if he had the money, he would not have been there to start with.

The veteran testified that following the surgery, he was still hurting and couldn't even walk, but on July 3, a different physician came into his room and said, "I'll be checking your surgery and your bandage." Such physician identified himself as in charge of urology. The veteran stated that the doctor he had been dealing with came in, but was sent back out by the physician who had identified himself as in charge of urology. Thereafter, he was taken down the hall to have his bandages changed and left the hospital on July 4. The veteran further testified that he was told by physicians prior to the surgery "that usually after they release someone from

ShutDownTheVA@gmail.com

the hospital and they come back after after four weeks they never see them any more." After the veteran returned to the Jackson VA Medical Center, his physician said, "you're swollen too much to tell anything right now" and that he would have to go home and come back on the next appointment. Such appointment was four weeks later, i.e., eight weeks after surgery; and, at that time, the physician tried pumping the prosthesis, but it wasn't working. The veteran indicated that he was told that the swelling had been fluctuating and the right side was swelling. He was told to come back after two weeks and when he asked to see a doctor before he left, he was told, "I am a doctor and I don't see nothing wrong with you. You're just a big old crybaby. Go home."

The veteran stated that he was home for a couple or three days and could hardly get up and get around. As such, he went to the Emergency Room at Forrest General Hospital. He underwent surgery to remove the pump. Following the surgery, he remained in the hospital for a week. Thereafter, he declined to return to the Jackson VA Medical Center because he had been lied to and used and instead went to the New Orleans VA Medical Center, where he was given antibiotics and told to come back in two or three weeks for follow-up. Subsequently, because he was still hurting, he went to the emergency room at the Biloxi VA Medical Center where he was admitted by the Urology Chief at Biloxi and placed on an IV to stabilize his condition prior to surgery. Thereafter, the veteran underwent surgery to remove the remaining portions of his penile prosthesis, except for the reservoir and a hose in his scrotum. The veteran stated that he remained in the Biloxi VA Medical Center for about three

ShutDownTheVA@gmail.com

weeks. The veteran testified that following the July 1996 surgery at the Jackson VA Medical Center, he noticed that his penis was smaller and he was in worse shape than prior to the surgery.

A VA genitourinary examination was conducted at the Louisville VA Medical Center in June 2001. The examiner stated that he had reviewed the veteran's extensive records prior to the examination. He also recorded a brief history of the veteran's current disability

Examination revealed a surgery scar in the right inguinal area. The veteran's penis was uncircumcised and normal in appearance, though there may be some fibrosis of the corpora cavernosa. Upon inquiry, the veteran was adamantly against another penile prosthesis. The examiner indicated that it might be impossible to restore him to normal physiologic function without the penile prosthesis, but that was what the veteran wanted.

Another VA genitourinary examination was conducted at the Louisville VA Medical Center in July 2001 and the examiner stated that she had made an extensive review of the veteran's records. She noted the veteran's history of being treated in 1996 at the Jackson VA Medical Center for erectile dysfunction, receiving a penile prosthesis. The veteran, at the July 2001 VA examination, claimed that his erectile dysfunction was worsened by the placement of the penile prosthesis and subsequent infection, requiring two surgical procedures to remove the infected hardware.

ShutDownTheVA@gmail.com

In response to the Board's inquiry as to whether the cited surgery created any additional disability after be performed in July 1996, the examiner stated that the veteran had preoperative psychiatric, spiritual, and genitourinary examinations, during which time he reported the complete absence of morning erections, inability to maintain erections, and premature ejaculation should he attain a modicum of erection during sexual stimulation. By the veteran's report, after his surgery he was rendered completely impotent. Based upon the preoperative evaluation, it was not evident that any or all of the surgical procedures either initiated in July 1996 or the subsequent removal of the hardware significantly changed his preexisting erectile dysfunction. The genitourinary examiner noted that on his evaluation in the spring of 1996, the veteran was noted not to be a good candidate for placement of a penile prosthesis due to some relatively unsophisticated impressions as to the quality and type of sexual function that would be possible after the procedure. She indicated that after some additional and extensive counseling, the veteran was then approved for placement of a penile prosthesis, which unfortunately became infected and required removal.

In response to the Board's request that the examiner identify the nature of the disorder prior to surgery and any additional disability, if any, after the surgery and it's relationship to the July 1996 penile prosthesis surgery, the genitourinary examiner noted that contemporaneous examination showed that the veteran had surgery scars in the right inguinal region, was uncircumcised, and had a normal appearing penis. It was also noted that there might be some fibrosis in the corpora cavernosa and that it might be impossible to restore him to

ShutDownTheVA@gmail.com

normal physiological function without the penile prosthesis due to the presence of scarring since his surgical procedure. The examiner specifically stated that the surgical procedures did not change the veteran's pre-existing condition.

At his personal hearing held in February 2002 before the undersigned traveling Veterans Law Judge of the Board of Veterans' Appeals, the veteran testified that in 1994 and 1995, he was having trouble maintaining an erection and that he started seeing a doctor at the Jackson VA Medical Center. He indicated that such physician gave him pills to help him sleep and other pills. He asked the doctor if that medication would cause a problem in sexual function, was informed that none of his medications would cause anything like that, and was referred to the urology clinic. He further testified that, when seen in the urology clinic, he explained that he was having problems with his foreskin swelling and obtaining a full erection. He was prescribed pills and subsequently obtained a VED pump. He related that the VED worked great, but if used twice in one night, would cause marked swelling in his foreskin that took days to go down. The veteran indicated that he explained the problem to physicians in the VA GU clinic, but they did not test him on his ability to use the pump. He was informed that a penile implant procedure was done at the Jackson VA Medical Center on a regular basis and that, if he had the procedure done, he wouldn't notice any difference with respect to size.

The veteran further testified that he was shown the components of the penile prosthesis by a physician, who demonstrated where all the parts would go. He also indicated that he underwent counseling with psychiatrist who told him

ShutDownTheVA@gmail.com

that this type of surgery is no longer a major problem and that he wouldn't notice any difference with respect to size. The veteran stated that he returned on July 1, 1996, to be examined by the anesthesia people and to sign some papers. He signed all three of the forms authorizing the surgery. In response to questioning from his representative, the veteran asserted that he chose the type of pump was ultimately implanted. He also testified that the doctors never explained what they were going to do, or the side effects, but told him that once the surgery was done, he would return after four weeks. The veteran further related that he was trying to read a piece of paper that explained to him how to use the penile prosthesis, but people who worked in urology kept coming in, asking him questions, and inquiring if he had signed particular documents. He stated that he asked to take "a bluish-green type colored sheet with a lot of fine type" upstairs to read, but was informed that the document was for the purpose of leaving his vehicle in the parking lot without it being towed, gets him on the meals list, and reserves his room. He stated that the next morning, he was prepped and taken to surgery, where the procedure was done Thereafter, he was taken to the recovery room and the following day, he was seen by a physician who identified himself as the man in charge of the urology clinic. The veteran testified that he was taken to have his wound washed and repacked and that he as in a lot of pain at that time. He was discharged on July 4, 1996 and, at that time, the nurse gave him a GU clinic appointment slip for four weeks after discharge. When he returned at that time, he was told to come back in two weeks because he was too swollen. He returned in two weeks for examination, but was sore and tender and the pump would not work. The veteran asserted that when he complained, he

ShutDownTheVA@gmail.com

was told that he was "just a big old crybaby and [to] go home." The veteran alleged that the Jackson VA Medical Center had implanted "a defective part" and that when that defective part failed to function, "they tried to send [him] on back down the road [hoping he] would die and they wouldn't have to put up with it."

The veteran further testified that he was seen in the Emergency Room of the Forrest General Hospital, where he underwent surgery to have the pump removed. He stated that he was also treated with antibiotics for a staph infection. Upon discharge, he went to the New Orleans VA Medical Center where he was given more antibiotics. The veteran also stated that he went to the Biloxi VA Medical Center where he underwent treatment with intravenous antibiotics and, subsequently, underwent removal of some of the penile prosthesis hardware, while capping the remainder. The veteran speculated concerning the actions and motivations of the professional staff at the Jackson VA Medical Center. He testified that he no longer had any infection, did not have any erections, did not have any pain or soreness, and had no difficulty voiding. He asserted that he had returned to Forrest General Hospital, where he was given shots to attempt to produce an erection, which were unsuccessful. He also stated that he had not been given encouragement that the condition can be improved and he continues to retain a portion of the device in his lower abdomen. The veteran indicated that he felt that the doctors at the Jackson VA Medical Center did not give him straight answers when the infection was setting in and the pump was defective. He was not willing to return to the Jackson VA Medical Center and that he has not kept

ShutDownTheVA@gmail.com

the appointments that they scheduled for him. A transcript of the testimony is of record.

In December 2002, the Office of the Regional Counsel indicated that the veteran's federal tort claim was denied on August 31, 1998. The veteran had alleged negligent care and treatment at the Jackson VA Medical Center involving penile implant. The claim was denied based upon a finding of no negligence. The appeal period expired February 28, 1999, with no appeal taken by the veteran.

Compliance with the Veterans Claims Assistance Act

On November 9, 2000, the VCAA was enacted. See 38 U.S.C.A. §§ 5103, 5103A (West 2002). Among other things, the VCAA amended 38 U.S.C.A. § 5103 to clarify VA's duty to notify claimants and their representatives of any information that is necessary to substantiate the claim for benefits. The VCAA also created 38 U.S.C.A. § 5103A, which codifies VA's duty to assist, and essentially states that VA will make reasonable efforts to assist a claimant in obtaining evidence necessary to substantiate a claim. Implementing regulations for the VCAA were subsequently enacted, which were also made effective November 9, 2000, for the most part. See 66 Fed. Reg. 45,620 (Aug. 29, 2001) (codified at 38 C.F.R. §§ 3.102, 3.159). The intended effect of the implementing regulations was to establish clear guidelines consistent with the intent of Congress regarding the timing and scope of assistance VA will provide to claimants who file a claim for benefits. See 66 Fed. Reg. 45,620 (Aug. 29, 2001). Both the VCAA and the implementing regulations are applicable in the present case,

ShutDownTheVA@gmail.com

and will be collectively referred to as "the VCAA."

To comply with the aforementioned VCAA requirements, the RO must satisfy the following four requirements. First, the RO must inform the claimant of the information and evidence not of record that is necessary to substantiate the claim. See 38 U.S.C.A. § 5103(West 2002) and 38 C.F.R. § 3.159(b)(1) (2004). A letter sent to the veteran in May 2001 informed him that, in order to establish entitlement to benefits under 38 U.S.C.A. § 1151, the evidence must show a current physical disability and a relationship between such disability and treatment from the VA Medical Center.

Second, the RO must inform the claimant of the information and evidence the VA will seek to provide. See 38 U.S.C.A. § 5103 (West 2002) and 38 C.F.R. § 3.159(b)(1) (2004). The May 2001 letter advised the veteran that VA would make reasonable efforts to help the veteran obtain evidence necessary to support his claim, to include medical records, employment records, or records from other Federal agencies. He was also notified that VA would obtain any VA medical records or other medical treatment records he identifies. The letter further informed the veteran that VA will assist him by providing a medical examination or obtaining a medical opinion if such is necessary to decide his claim.

Third, the RO must inform the claimant of the information and evidence the claimant is expected to provide. See 38 U.S.C.A. § 5103 (West 2002) and 38 C.F.R. § 3.159(b)(1) (2004). The May 2001 letter notified the veteran that he needed to submit evidence that establishes a relationship

ShutDownTheVA@gmail.com

between his current disability and treatment from VA care providers. He was further informed that if he would like VA to obtain additional evidence or information in support of his claim, he should identify it. The letter also described the type of evidence that may be used to support his claim, to include medical or other evidence showing that he has persistent recurrent symptoms of a disability, statements from the veteran or other individuals describing his physical disability symptoms, and medical records or medical opinions demonstrating a relationship between a current disability and VA treatment.

Finally, the RO must request that the claimant provide any evidence in the claimant's possession that pertains to the claim. See 38 U.S.C.A. § 5103 (West 2002) and 38 C.F.R. § 3.159(b)(1) (2004). Even though the RO never sent a letter specifically requesting that the veteran provide any evidence in his possession that pertained to his claim (as required by 38 C.F.R. § 3.159 (b)), the Board finds that the veteran is not prejudiced by such failure. The May 2001 letter did request the veteran to send the RO information describing additional evidence or the evidence itself. Moreover, the RO has consistently requested the veteran provide information about where and by whom he was treated for his claimed disability. Moreover, the veteran has not identified any additional outstanding relevant medical evidence to be considered in connection with his 38 U.S.C.A. § 1151 claim. Therefore, for all of the aforementioned reasons, it is determined that the veteran was not prejudiced by the RO's not specifically requesting that the veteran provide any evidence in his possession that pertained to his claim.

ShutDownTheVA@gmail.com

Additionally, the September 1998 statement of the case, as well as the supplemental statements of the case issued in June 1999, November 1999, September 2001, and November 2004 further advised the veteran of the evidence considered, the adjudicative actions taken, the pertinent laws and regulations regarding claims for benefits under 38 U.S.C.A. § 1151, the decision reached, and the reasons and base for such decision. Moreover, the November 2004 supplemental statement of the case provided the veteran with regulations pertaining to the VCAA, as well as the cites to the United States Code for such regulations.

In short, the RO has informed the veteran of the information and evidence not of record that is needed, the information and evidence that the VA will seek to provide, and the information and evidence the veteran must provide. See 38 U.S.C.A. § 5103 (West 2002) and 38 C.F.R. § 3.159(b)(1) (2004); Quartuccio v. Principi, 16 Vet.App. 183 (2002).

In view of the procedures that have been undertaken in this claim, further development is not needed to comply with VCAA. The veteran has been informed of the information and evidence needed to substantiate his claim, and he has been made aware of how VA would assist him in obtaining evidence and information. He has not identified any additional, relevant evidence that has not been requested or obtained. The veteran has also been afforded VA examinations for the purpose of adjudicating his claim. For the aforementioned reasons, there is no reasonable possibility that further assistance would aid in the substantiation of the claim.

ShutDownTheVA@gmail.com

Analysis

The veteran claims entitlement to 38 U.S.C.A. § 1151 benefits
for erectile dysfunction as a consequence of surgical treatment at the Jackson VA Medical Center. He asserts that the surgery required two days rather than the customary one and he continuously experienced pain and swelling. As a result, he entered Forrest General Hospital, a private facility in Hattiesburg, Mississippi, where the pump was removed. Thereafter, he was treated with pills at the New Orleans VA Medical Center and ultimately, on September 5, 1996, had additional tubes removed at the Biloxi VA Medical Center. The veteran contends that he has been permanently severely impaired as a result of the damage done at the Jackson VA Medical Center.

The veteran's claim for benefits based upon erectile dysfunction is premised on 38 U.S.C.A. § 1151. Because the claim was filed in July 1997, the version of § 1151 that is applicable to this case is the version that existed prior to its amendment in 1996, as those amendments were made applicable only to claims filed on or after October 1, 1997. See Pub. L. No. 104-204, § 422(b)(1), (c), 110 Stat. 2926-27 (1996).

The pre-amendment version of § 1151 provides, in relevant part:
Where any veteran shall have suffered an injury, or an aggravation of an injury, as the result of hospitalization, medical or surgical treatment, or the pursuit of a course of vocational rehabilitation under chapter 31 of this title,

ShutDownTheVA@gmail.com

awarded under any of the laws administered by the Secretary, or as a result of having submitted to an examination under any such law, and not the result of such veterans own willful misconduct, and such injury or aggravation results in additional disability to or the death of such veteran, disability or death compensation under this chapter and dependency and indemnity compensation under chapter 13 of this title shall be awarded in the same manner as if such disability, aggravation, or death were service-connected. 38 U.S.C.A. § 1151 (in effect prior to October 1, 1997). All claims for benefits under § 1151 filed prior to October 1, 1997 must be adjudicated under the provisions of § 1151 as they existed prior to that date. VAOPGCPREC 40-97.

The regulatory framework developed by the VA to implement 38 U.S.C.A. § 1151 is contained at 38 C.F.R. § 3.358. Prior to November 1991, the VA had long interpreted 38 U.S.C.A. § 1151 to require a showing of fault on the part of the VA or the occurrence of an accident to establish entitlement to compensation under § 1151 for adverse consequences of VA medical treatment based on the regulatory provision found at 38 C.F.R. § 3.358(c)(3), (4).

However, on November 25, 1991, in the case of Gardner v. Derwinski, 1 Vet. App. 584 (1991), the Court invalidated 38 C.F.R. § 3.358(c)(3), holding that that portion of the regulation was unlawful because it exceeded the authority of the Secretary of the VA and violated the statutory rights granted to veterans by Congress under § 1151. The Secretary appealed the decision to the U.S. Court of Appeals for the Federal Circuit (Federal Circuit), and eventually to the U.S. Supreme Court (Supreme Court). In April 1992, pending the

ShutDownTheVA@gmail.com

completion of appellate review and litigation, the VA administratively stayed consideration of all claims for benefits under 38 U.S.C.A. § 1151.

The Federal Circuit subsequently concluded that the VA's regulations interpreting § 1151 as requiring fault or accident were entitled to no deference and held that 38 C.F.R. § 3.358(c)(3) was invalid. Gardner v. Brown, 5 F.3d 1456 (Fed. Cir. 1993). On December 12, 1994, the Supreme Court similarly held that the VA was not authorized by § 1151 to exclude from compensation the "contemplated or foreseeable" results of non-negligent medical treatment, as provided by 38 C.F.R. § 3.358(c)(3). Brown v. Gardner, 513 U.S. 115, 115 S.Ct. 552, 130 L.Ed.2d. 462 (1994).

On March 16, 1995, amended regulations which conformed to the Supreme Court's decision were published, effective retroactively to November 25, 1991. The fault or accident requirement of 38 C.F.R. § 3.358(c)(3) was deleted; 38 C.F.R. § 3.358(c)(3) now provides that compensation is not payable for the "necessary consequences" of proper treatment to which the veteran consented. The final regulatory amendments were adopted on May 23, 1996, and codified at 38 C.F.R. § 3.358(c), effective July 22, 1996.

Based upon the foregoing, it is clear that in order to prevail, the claimant must establish that he "suffered an injury, or an aggravation of an injury, as the result of hospitalization, medical or surgical treatment", . . . not the result of such veteran's own willful misconduct, and [that] "such injury or aggravation results in additional disability to or the death of such veteran."

ShutDownTheVA@gmail.com

The Board finds that the veteran is not entitled to benefits under 38 U.S.C.A. § 1151 as the medical evidence establishes that the veteran suffered erectile dysfunction with inability to achieve or maintain an erection sufficient to have intercourse prior to the July 2, 1996, surgery and there is no evidence of additional disability as a result of such surgical procedure.

The Board notes that the veteran was evaluated in the Sexual Dysfunction Clinic on June 15, 1995, at which time he reported a gradual onset of decreased ability to obtain and maintain an erection sufficient for intercourse for about one year. He further related that that he was able to obtain erections sufficient for intercourse roughly 30 percent of the time during the last year, but denied morning or nocturnal erections during the past year. VA outpatient treatment records, dated in July 1995, show that the veteran was seen in the GU clinic for erectile dysfunction, while VA outpatient treatment records, dated in January 1996, show that the veteran was being followed for erectile dysfunction and that he had bought a vacuum device, but that its use caused pain and a "blood knot" on use.

In addition, VA outpatient treatment records from the Sexual Dysfunction Consultation Clinic at the Jackson VA Medical Center, dated in February 1996, show that the veteran was referred by the GU clinic for presenting complaints of erectile dysfunction for approximately 10 years. He veteran stated that this condition has gradually worsened, particularly in the past few years, and that currently he was unable to attain a firm erection (including nocturnal

ShutDownTheVA@gmail.com

erections) despite intact sexual desire. The veteran reported that he has had a number of girlfriends, but has been unable to maintain a relationship due to his sexual dysfunction. The diagnoses were sexual dysfunction, not otherwise stated; and premature ejaculation. VA outpatient treatment records, dated in June 1996, show that the veteran was being followed for erectile dysfunction for one year, and had been cleared by psychology for a penile implant.

The veteran's arguments devoted to whether he had erectile dysfunction 5 or 10 years prior to the surgical procedure performed on July 2, 1996, are beside the point, as the evidence of record, including his own statements and the clinical findings, clearly show that he experienced an established erectile dysfunction, with inability to achieve or maintain an erection sufficient to have intercourse, for a period of at least one year prior to that procedure. Furthermore, the evidence demonstrates that the veteran received VA outpatient treatment for such condition, all remedial efforts had been unavailing, and that he independently obtained information regarding the process of penile prosthesis implantation.

Based upon the foregoing, the Board finds that the veteran experienced erectile dysfunction, with inability to achieve or maintain an erection sufficient to have intercourse, prior to the penile prosthesis implant performed on July 2, 1996. His current assertions that his former use of the VED was "great" conflicts with a January 1996 medical record that shows that the veteran had bought a vacuum device, but that its use caused pain and a "blood knot" on use, as well as the assessment of "pain and hematoma with vacuum device," and the February 1996 record from the Sexual Dysfunction Consultation Clinic showing that the veteran had been treated with Yocon pills and a vacuum tumescence pump, but was not satisfied with the results of either treatment. Thus, the clear preponderance of the evidence is against a finding that the veteran functioned well with a VED before his implant surgery.

The Board further finds that the veteran's claims that he was not provided adequate information, or was "lied to," regarding his penile prosthesis implant are without merit. To the contrary, VA outpatient treatment records, dated in January 1996, show that the reporting physician stated that he discussed a penile prosthetic implant with the veteran. He further noted that the veteran had sent for literature on a penile prosthesis implant on his own. To the same point, the February 1996 VA treatment records from the Sexual Dysfunction Consultation Clinic show that it was noted to be important to ensure that the veteran has realistic expectations regarding the effects of the surgery on both erectile and orgasmic function. Moreover, at the time of his July 1996 penile implant surgery, the veteran signed a consent form indicating that he had been made aware of the nature and purpose of the operation or procedure, the possible alternative methods of treatment, the risks involved, and the possibility of complications. Such document also indicates that the veteran had been informed of the risks of death, infection, bleeding, erosion, removal of prosthesis, penile shortening, and penile, urethral, and bladder damage.

ShutDownTheVA@gmail.com

Additionally, the medical evidence of record fails to establish the clinical presence of additional disability as a result of the surgical procedure at the Jackson VA Medical Center on July 2, 1996. Specifically, the Board observes that, in response to inquiry as to whether the surgery created any additional disability, the July 2001 VA examiner opined that the veteran had preoperative psychiatric, spiritual, and genitourinary examinations, during which he reported the complete absence of morning erections, inability to maintain erections, and premature ejaculation should he attain a modicum of erection during sexual stimulation. By the veteran's report, after his surgery he was rendered completely impotent. Based upon the preoperative evaluation, the examiner concluded that it was not evident that any or all of the surgical procedures either initiated in July 1996 or the subsequent removal of the hardware significantly changed his preexisting erectile dysfunction.

Based upon the foregoing, the Board finds that the veteran the veteran suffered erectile dysfunction with inability to achieve or maintain an erection sufficient to have intercourse for a period of approximately one year prior to the July 1996 penile implant surgery and that, following such surgery and resulting infection, the veteran had erectile dysfunction with inability to achieve or maintain an erection sufficient to have intercourse. Moreover, there is no evidence of record detailing additional disability as a result of the July 1996 surgery.

In the absence of objective clinical evidence showing that the veteran's established erectile dysfunction underwent any

ShutDownTheVA@gmail.com

aggravation of his preexisting erectile dysfunction as a result of VA surgical treatment on July 2, 1996, the veteran is not entitled to benefits under the provisions of 38 U.S.C.A. § 1151.

ORDER

Entitlement to benefits under the provisions of 38 U.S.C.A. § 1151 for disability resulting from surgical treatment at a VA medical facility on July 2, 1996, is **denied**.

G. H. Shufelt
Veterans Law Judge, Board of Veterans' Appeals
Department of Veterans Affairs

ShutDownTheVA@gmail.com

Death

ShutDownTheVA@gmail.com

Story #5

2019

Homicide at the VA[9]

Reprinted with permission of USA Today. Thank you for taking care of veterans, those who serve to protect you. Please visit their website to say thanks. www.usatoday.com

---

'I trusted those people.' Red flags missed, limiting evidence in potential serial killer case at VA hospital

---

[9] https://www.usatoday.com/story/news/investigations/2019/10/15/clarksburgvadaths-hospital-oversights-lapses-limit-homicide-evidence/3922640002/

ShutDownTheVA@gmail.com

You have no doubt read about death occurring at Veterans Administration facilities over the years, accidental or otherwise?

This tragic story of loss at the VA is even more disgusting. Read on.

CLARKSBURG, W.Va. – 5 of 5 11/20/2019, 10:31 AM
It was 1:55 a.m., and Felix "Kirk" McDermott was struggling to breathe. He was cold and clammy. A doctor called to his bedside at the Veterans Affairs hospital in Clarksburg, West Virginia, noted white foam oozing from the 82-year-old's mouth and a crackling sound coming from his lungs. McDermott's heart was racing; his pupils were pinpoints. Seemingly out of the blue, the Vietnam veteran's blood sugar had plummeted dangerously – to one-sixth the level that triggers urgent treatment, medical records show.

That dramatic decline could have been a significant clue, since McDermott was not diabetic. But it was not recognized as such in the early morning hours of April 9, 2018.

It was just one in a string of oversights at the Louis A. Johnson VA Medical Center that risked, and may have cost, other veterans' lives. Now, those missed opportunities limit the evidence available to prosecutors as they seek to build a criminal case. **Family members said investigators told them they are** focusing on a person of interest who may have killed as many as **10 patients in** 11 months by injecting them with insulin. "When someone has intention to do harm in these settings, they will take advantage of any loopholes, any opportunities to exploit the system," said Elizabeth Yardley, a criminology professor at Birmingham City University in England who has studied nurses convicted of murder. "It can be an investigative nightmare."

Hospital spokesman Wesley Walls said officials notified authorities "immediately upon discovering these serious allegations" and put "safeguards in place to ensure the safety of each and every one of our patients." The person has been removed from patient care. Events before and after McDermott's death suggest numerous lapses in medical diligence.

Nurses quickly began treating his symptoms, giving him glucose. But medical records do not indicate that anyone ordered a blood test that could have detected the unprescribed insulin investigators suspect coursed through his veins, killing him.

After he died, no one at the hospital ordered an autopsy despite the mysterious drop in blood sugar. Insulin on the ward wasn't adequately tracked, so there was no easy way to tell whether any was missing that night, employees said. In fact, they said, insulin was routinely left unsecured, violating the hospital's own policies. Complicating matters further, Unit 3A had no video surveillance to document the movement of its insulin – or its employees.

McDermott was the second of three men to die under similar circumstances over three days. Yet no one tipped off authorities that something was amiss for two and a half months, even as the death toll continued to climb, on the same ward, in the same way. High-risk insulin left out,

ShutDownTheVA@gmail.com

violating policy Insulin saves lives by keeping blood sugar in check, whether produced naturally in our bodies or administered, as with diabetics. But too much can be deadly. Symptoms of overdose include cold sweats and a fast heartbeat, as well as confusion and loss of consciousness. McDermott suffered from dementia, so confusion might have been hard to diagnose. But his heart was racing and, when his daughter arrived at his bedside before dawn, she found him drifting in and out of consciousness. He was the only patient in a room near the end of a hallway, on the third-floor medical surgical unit known as 3A.

For four hours, McDermott's blood sugar fluctuated, out of control. Nursing staff checked it every 15 minutes, his records show. When they gave him glucose, it shot up, then tanked again. "You had like a couple minutes that he'd talk to you, then he'd be back like he was sleeping," his daughter, Melanie Proctor, recalled. "Sometimes you could give his arm a shake, or, you know, 'Hey dad, are you going to talk to us?' and sometimes he would and other times, he wouldn't."

VA Inspector General Michael Missal has said his office is working with the FBI to investigate potential wrongdoing resulting in patient deaths at the hospital. His office declined to provide any details, as have the FBI and Department of Justice, saying they want to protect the integrity of the investigation.

Family members interviewed by investigators said they were told a person of interest may have been responsible for injecting the insulin that killed as many as 10 patients on

ShutDownTheVA@gmail.com

Unit 3A, a scope confirmed by someone familiar with the investigation. The deaths under investigation span the last half of 2017 through July 2018.

"These guys were dying the exact same way, one after another," said personal injury attorney Tony O'Dell. "It's inconceivable that the hospital staff wouldn't recognize this pattern and prevent the next one."

But pinpointing where the insulin came from will be challenging.

The Joint Commission, which accredits a majority of hospitals across the country – including the more than 150 VAs that treat about 9 million veterans annually – flagged insulin nearly 20 years ago as a "high-alert" medication, one of five with the "highest risk of causing injury when misused." The commission requires hospitals to manage the medications safely.

The VA has labeled insulin a "high-risk" medication since at least 2002 and requires its hospitals to take "all necessary actions to reduce the likelihood of intentional or unintentional untoward use."

The agency lets each hospital create its own policies, so practices vary widely.

At the VA hospital in Clarksburg, policies dating to 2015 list insulin among high-risk medications that "must be stored in a locked area." A memo signed by hospital director Glenn Snider on Feb. 10, 2018, directs that "all drugs stored in the

ShutDownTheVA@gmail.com

ward and clinic areas will be kept locked in medication carts, cabinets or medication rooms."

Yet on Unit 3A, insulin routinely was left unsecured on hallway medication carts, according to two hospital employees who spoke on condition of anonymity for fear of retaliation. One of them offered details: Insulin was left on top of the carts, the carts weren't locked or the locks weren't working.

Walls, the hospital spokesman, said it is not accurate that insulin was routinely left unsecured in violation of hospital policy. Insulin, he added, can be purchased at drug stores without a prescription.

"Also, it's important to note that regulations and protocols can only do so much to protect against criminal activity," Walls said.

Since the flurry of deaths last year, the Clarksburg VA has improved its insulin monitoring. A policy updated in September requires that two people be present when insulin is retrieved from locked medication cabinets, according to copies of internal directives obtained by USA TODAY.

Another, governing operation of medication carts, was issued April 2 and signed by Paul Carter, the hospital's associate director for patient care services. It said nursing staff would be issued six-digit PIN codes for the carts.

"Once the medication(s) has been retrieved," the policy warns, "you MUST ensure all drawers are closed and the

ShutDownTheVA@gmail.com

medication cart is locked."

Amid cluster of deaths, failure to detect a pattern
As McDermott's body lay lifeless after the hours-long struggle to save him, staff placed a frame on his gurney and draped an American flag on top.

The hospital chaplain was summoned to say a prayer. A recording of taps played as workers slowly rolled the veteran away. Nursing staff and others stopped what they were doing. Some stood at attention, others offered their thoughts on the deceased.

"Anybody that had dealt with him that night ... said something, you know, 'I'm sorry for your loss,' " recalled Proctor, McDermott's daughter. "I can remember one of them saying, 'Your dad had one heck of a sense of humor.' " The flag tradition is known as a "final salute." It played out the same way the next day for George Nelson Shaw Sr., 81, an Air Force veteran and avid bowler, who also had suffered a bout of acute low blood sugar.

The VA follows many similar traditions. And it is bound by thousands of regulations, including strict protocols to avoid patterns of failure.

When a major incident causes a patient harm, hospital leaders are required to file a report in a national database.

That information, kept confidential, is gathered to develop lessons for the nationwide health care system.

ShutDownTheVA@gmail.com

Felix "Kirk" McDermott, 82, was one of four veterans to die within 16 days after unexplained low-blood sugar at the VA hospital in Clarksburg, West Virginia.

Such incidents are supposed to be designated "sentinel events."

More than 1 million of these "root-cause" analyses and accompanying safety reports have been entered into the system since it was established, according to the VA.

At the Clarksburg hospital, the cluster of unexpected patient deaths after acute low-blood sugar episodes apparently triggered no such reporting or inquiry. In addition to Shaw and McDermott, William Alfred Holloway, 96, and Army veteran Archie Edgell, 84, all died within a 16-day period.

Weeks after the last of those deaths, inspectors visited the hospital for a routine care review. They noted the hospital had not designated a single event as sentinel in the prior 32 months.

The inspectors cited a half-dozen serious episodes over that time that they said should have been flagged as possible sentinel events. They said administrators failed to report other major medical problems and to disclose the information to patients and their families.

A month after that visit, in June 2018, a group of Clarksburg A doctors brought concerns about the deaths to the hospital's patient safety staff, according to a timeline released by Sen.

Joe Manchin, D-W.Va. The safety staff notified the hospital director, who called VA headquarters in Washington.

The inspector general's office again sent out inspectors, who arrived at the beginning of July – as the suspected death toll reached 10.

When asked about reporting delays, Walls, the hospital spokesman, said, "VA's independent inspector general has been investigating this issue for longer than it took (hospital staff) to identify it." He referred questions about "specific timelines" to investigators.

Missal, the VA inspector general, said federal authorities "have been working with urgency to complete the investigation.

The families and the public deserve nothing less."

Insulin tests came months late, after blood evidence was drained. Proving homicides by insulin injection can be difficult with even the best evidence. At the Clarksburg VA, tests for insulin came months later when bodies were exhumed – after potential blood evidence had been drained and bodies embalmed.

One veteran had been cremated.
The doctor called to McDermott's bedside early on the morning of April 9 had ordered a chest X-ray and a diuretic in case of fluid buildup in his lungs, medical records show. He was placed on a machine to help him breathe. The doctor ordered blood tests that confirmed McDermott's sugar and

ShutDownTheVA@gmail.com

oxygen levels were low. But, according to a copy of the medical records provided to USA TODAY, those tests did not measure insulin or a key amino acid – C-peptide – that specialists said could have detected the unprescribed insulin. "If people don't have diabetes, they should do that (test)," said Adrian Vella, professor of medicine at the Mayo Clinic and author of a literature review on the topic. "You're supposed to check glucose ... and you're supposed to get an insulin and C-peptide."

Other specialists said providers may not routinely order such tests if other factors could help explain low blood sugar levels, such as liver problems, infection or other medications. Washington University School of Medicine professor emeritus Philip Cryer said such factors wouldn't explain McDermott's "profound hypoglycemia all of a sudden."

"You could not explain that absent measurements of insulin and C-peptide," said Cryer, who co-wrote clinical guidelines for evaluating low-blood sugar disorders. "Ideally, those should have been measured."

McDermott had been admitted to Unit 3A three days earlier with a fever and cough. He had heart problems along with his dementia. Medical staff diagnosed him with pneumonia from inhaled food.He had been responding to antibiotics and, the day before his death, a doctor noted in his chart that he was "much more alert and talking with family." His blood-sugar level was normal – until suddenly it wasn't. By 6 a.m., after staff had tried for four hours to stabilize McDermott without success, Proctor and other family members told them to stop medical intervention, to let him go.

ShutDownTheVA@gmail.com

When he died three hours later, his daughter said, the family didn't request an autopsy because "we thought he had passed on his own, natural causes."

Possible autopsy criteria itemized in McDermott's medical record include "unexpected or unexplained" death "when clinical course seemed to be improving." Staff did not indicate that he met that criteria.

Even if the family had asked for an autopsy, it's unclear whether an examination at the hospital would have revealed anything untoward. When Shaw passed away the next day, a hospital autopsy requested by his family concluded he had died from heart failure.

Both deaths later were **reclassified as homicides** after federal investigators launched their probe.

McDermott's remains were exhumed six months after his death, in October 2018, and sent to Dover Air Force Base for an autopsy. An armed forces medical examiner identified an injection site in his abdomen that tested positive for insulin.

On Shaw's body, exhumed and re-autopsied in January, the examiner found four insulin injection sites – two on the left arm, one on the right and another on his right thigh.

Like McDermott, Shaw had no history of diabetes or prescribed insulin. The examiner concluded both men had been killed by insulin injection.

ShutDownTheVA@gmail.com

Walls, the hospital spokesman, declined to comment on blood tests and autopsies performed at the hospital, again referring questions to investigators.

Michelle Aurelius, a member of the Autopsy Committee with the College of American Pathologists, said the scope of hospital and medical examiner autopsies differ, even though the methods are similar.

A hospital autopsy typically looks for evidence of disease in a natural death to provide explanations for physicians and families. A forensic autopsy focuses on sudden, unexpected and possibly violent death, with a goal of determining the manner and cause while gathering evidence for law enforcement.

Since insulin needles are tiny, Aurelius said, it "may be very difficult or impossible to find an injection site."

Howard Robin, a California pathologist, said initial autopsies may detect needle marks, but pathologists "must have a significant level of suspicion to make the diagnosis" of homicide by insulin injection.

Clarksburg spellbound by 'Twilight Zone' whodunit
News of the 10 suspicious deaths and speculation about the person of interest who investigators believe may be responsible for them has roiled the city of Clarksburg, West Virginia. The VA hospital is one of the largest employers in the area with 1,000 workers, and it draws patients from across the region. Signs outside the Louis A. Johnson VA Medical Center clearly state its mission. One notes that the

hospital "honors our heroes," another that "the price of freedom is visible here."

Inside, there is no indication of the pall cast by the recent headlines. A lobby shop stocks black and gold Steelers gear, women's shoes and snacks. Medical workers in scrubs counsel a veteran in the emergency room lobby and wish visitors in hallways a good day.

Nearly everywhere else, news of the deaths has gripped the city of Clarksburg since it became public in August when the first legal action, a wrongful death claim seeking $6 million on behalf of McDermott, was filed by Tony O'Dell. The VA hospital has a huge footprint here. It is among the economically depressed area's biggest employers, with 1,000 workers, and draws patients from across the region, serving about 70,000 veterans in north central West Virginia and nearby Maryland, Ohio and Pennsylvania. O'Dell, a partner in a firm in the state capital, also represents other victims' families in the case. He blames the Clarksburg VA for failures both systemic and pervasive. O'Dell says the hospital breached its duty to warn patients and their families.

"There is simply no excuse whatsoever for these deaths to have gone on for so long," he said. "That is an insult to these veterans' families, and they should be ashamed."

At a Panera Bread restaurant on the edge of Clarksburg, Norma Shaw fights back tears as she talks about her husband's death. She is angry – at the possible assailant, at the hospital, at the VA in general.

ShutDownTheVA@gmail.com

"I trusted those people, I did," she said.
McDermott's daughter feels the same way.
"I'm still very angry – still very, very angry," she said.

Veterans who gathered to hear a band on a recent Thursday at the American Legion Post 13 lamented that the case turned a national spotlight on the town, for all the wrong reasons.

"It just breaks our hearts," said Michael Greaver, the post's commander. "It's so bad for morale in our community."
Behind the bar, Susie Jimenez doled out Budweisers and pull-tab raffle tickets. She sees the outside attention a little differently, saying she hopes the pressure continues until "justice is served for these veterans."

Jimenez criticized the hospital for not telling the public for 14 months after the investigation was launched, saying, "It shouldn't have been swept under the rug."

Walls said investigators instructed the hospital not to share information with anyone outside the inspector general's office. The hospital told employees not to speak with the news media either. Many doctors, nurses and nursing assistants who worked on 3A at the time of the deaths declined to comment or failed to respond to messages left at their homes.

When a reporter visited a residence listed for the person of interest in public records, a man outside accepted a handwritten note seeking comment, but no one got back in touch. Speculation about the person ripples through conversations in town these days. *USA TODAY* is not identifying them because authorities have not named or charged anyone. But locally, pictures of a former hospital employee have been posted and discussed online.

Back at the American Legion hall, Greaver – an Iraq War veteran with 17 years' active duty in the Army and Navy – said he has received medical care at the hospital for years. "I walk the halls of that hospital, and there's family members, friends everywhere," he said.

"It's very unfortunate that an Alfred Hitchcock episode – "Twilight Zone" episode – happened here," he said. "Now everybody's asking questions, across America."

Contributing: Ken Alltucker

ShutDownTheVA@gmail.com

Story #6

2019

Robert Morris Levy

Here is press release from the Western District Office of the U.S. Attorney's Office about a "serial killer" that was arrested in August 2019. Levy was the longtime chief pathologist at Veterans Health Care System of the Ozarks in Fayetteville, Ark. I call him "serial killer" because of an ongoing and disgusting pattern of behavior towards veterans who died on his watch.

U.S. Attorneys » Western District of Arkansas » News
Share
Department of Justice
U.S. Attorney's Office
Western District of Arkansas

FOR IMMEDIATE RELEASE
Tuesday, August 20, 2019

ShutDownTheVA@gmail.com

Fayetteville Doctor Arrested On Charges Of Wire Fraud, Mail Fraud, Making False Statements, And Involuntary Manslaughter[10]

Fayetteville, Arkansas – Duane (DAK) Kees, United States Attorney for the Western District of Arkansas and Michael Missal, Inspector General of the Department of Veterans Affairs, announced today that **Robert Morris Levy** was arrested on federal charges stemming from a year-long investigation. A federal grand jury in the Western District of Arkansas indicted **Levy** on twelve counts of wire fraud, twelve counts of mail fraud, four counts of making false statements in certain matters, and three counts of involuntary manslaughter.

According to the Indictment, **Levy** held a medical license issued by the Mississippi State Board of Medical Licensure issued in 1997. In 2005, the Veterans Health Care System of the Ozarks ("Fayetteville VA") hired **Levy** to serve as the Chief of Pathology and Laboratory Medical Services, a position he held until his termination in 2018.

In 2015, **Levy** was interviewed by an administrative fact-finding panel regarding reports that **Levy** was under the influence of alcohol while on duty. **Levy** denied the allegations. In 2016, **Levy** appeared to be intoxicated while on duty, and a subsequent drug and alcohol test revealed **Levy's** blood alcohol content was .396.0 mg/dL. As a result,

---

[10] https://www.justice.gov/usao-wdar/pr/fayetteville-doctor-arrested-charges-wire-fraud-mail-fraud-making-false-statements-and

the Fayetteville VA summarily suspended **Levy's** privileges to practice medicine and issued **Levy** a written notice of removal and revocation of clinical privileges. **Levy** acknowledged that the pending proposed removal and revocation of clinical privileges was "due to unprofessional conduct related to high blood alcohol content while on duty" and in July 2016, **Levy** voluntarily entered a three-month in-patient treatment program, which he completed in October 2016.

Toward the end of the treatment program, **Levy** executed a contract with the Mississippi Physician Health Program and the Mississippi State Board of Medical Licensure in anticipation of returning to practice medicine at the Fayetteville VA. In the contract, **Levy** agreed to maintain sobriety to ensure his ability to practice medicine with reasonable skill and safety to patients. **Levy** agreed to "abstain completely from the use of . . . alcohol and other mood-altering substances" and to submit to random urine and/or blood drug screens. Non-compliance would potentially subject **Levy** to loss of his medical license and, in turn, his employment by the Fayetteville VA. **Levy** returned to work at the Fayetteville VA in October 2016.

As part of the contract, **Levy** randomly provided urine specimens and blood samples for drug testing from November 2016 through June 2018. Each blood sample and urine specimen tested was reported negative for the presence of drugs and alcohol. On twelve occasions beginning in June 2017 and continuing through 2018, while **Levy** was contractually obligated to submit to random drug and alcohol screens, **Levy** purchased for personal consumption 2-

methyl-2-butanol (2M-2B), a chemical substance that enables a person to achieve a state of intoxication but is not detectable in routine drug and alcohol testing methodology.

The Indictment charges that **Levy** devised a scheme to defraud the Department of Veterans Affairs (VA) and to obtain money and property from the VA in the form of salary, benefits, and performance awards he would not have received had the VA known **Levy** was intentionally concealing his non-compliance with the drug and alcohol testing program. In furtherance of this scheme, **Levy** concealed a material fact and made material false and fraudulent representations.

The Indictment also alleges that **Levy** twice made false statements to a special agent of the Office of the Inspector General of the Department of Veterans Affairs. The Indictment further alleges that **Levy** made false statements in health care matters by entering information in a patient's medical records that **Levy** knew to be false and by making a false statement during a grievance hearing related to his employment.

Finally, the Indictment charges **Levy** with three counts of involuntary manslaughter for causing the death of three patients through entering incorrect and misleading diagnoses and, on two occasions, by falsifying entries in the patients' medical records to state that a second pathologist concurred with the diagnosis **Levy** had made. The Indictment alleges that the incorrect and misleading diagnoses rendered by **Levy** caused the deaths of three veterans.

Duane (DAK) Kees, the United States Attorney for the Western District of Arkansas stated, "This indictment should remind us all that this country has a responsibility to care for those who have served us honorably. When that trust is violated through criminal conduct, those responsible must be held accountable. Our veterans deserve nothing less."

"The arrest of Dr. Levy was accomplished as a result of the strong leadership of the US Attorney's Office and the extensive work of special agents of the VA Office of Inspector General, supported by the medical expertise of the OIG's healthcare inspection professionals," stated Michael Missal, Inspector General of the Department of Veterans Affairs. "These charges send a clear signal that anyone entrusted with the care of veterans will be held accountable for placing them at risk by working while impaired or through other misconduct. Our thoughts are with the veterans and their families affected by Dr. Levy's actions." United States Magistrate Judge Erin L. Wiedemann presided over **Levy's** arraignment today.

The Department of Veterans Affairs Office of Inspector General is conducting the investigation and Assistant United States Attorneys Kyra Jenner and Bryan Achorn are prosecuting the case for the United States.

An Indictment is merely an accusation. An arrest warrant represents a finding of probable cause. A person is presumed innocent unless or until he or she is proven guilty beyond a reasonable doubt in a court of law.

ShutDownTheVA@gmail.com

Story #7

2019

The loss of even one person because of neglect or incompetence is horrific. So, now let me show you such an example. In this press release from the Massachusetts office of the Department of Justice, a VA employee did not do her job and a patient died.

U.S. Attorneys » District of Massachusetts » News
Department of Justice
U.S. Attorney's Office
District of Massachusetts

FOR IMMEDIATE RELEASE
Friday, November 15, 2019

Former Bedford VA Nursing Assistant Sentenced for Making False Statements [11]

---

[11] https://www.justice.gov/usao-ma/pr/former-bedford-va-nursing-assistant-sentenced-making-false-statements

Defendant lied about conducting hourly bed checks of VA patient who died

BOSTON – A former nursing assistant at the Veterans Affairs (VA) Medical Center in Bedford was sentenced today in federal court in Boston for making false statements to federal agents in connection with an investigation of a patient's death.

Patricia A. Waible, 52, of Nashua, N.H., was sentenced by U.S. District Court Judge F. Dennis Saylor IV to one year of probation. In July 2019, Waible was charged and agreed to plead guilty to two counts of making false statements.

On July 3, 2016, Waible, a nursing assistant at the time, worked the overnight shift from midnight to 8:00 a.m. at the Bedford VA's nursing home unit. During the shift, Waible's responsibilities included conducting hourly bed checks.

Early that morning, a patient who suffered from several serious medical ailments was found unresponsive and not breathing. The patient was transferred by ambulance to an emergency room, where he was later pronounced dead. During the ensuing investigation, on two separate occasions, Waible falsely stated to federal agents that she had conducted the hourly checks on the patient during her shift. United States Attorney Andrew E. Lelling; Joseph R. Bonavolonta, Special Agent in Charge of the Federal Bureau of Investigation, Boston Field Division; and Sean Smith, Special Agent in Charge of the Department of Veterans Affairs Office of Inspector General, Criminal Investigations Division, made the announcement today. Assistant U.S.

ShutDownTheVA@gmail.com

Attorneys Amanda P.M. Strachan, Chief of Lelling's Health Care Fraud Unit, and William B. Brady, also of Lelling's Health Care Fraud Unit, prosecuted the case.

ShutDownTheVA@gmail.com

Surgery

ShutDownTheVA@gmail.com

Story #8

2015

I doubt you have ever heard a story like this one. It comes from Contributor Cat del Valle Castellanos at the Huffington Post. Cat writes about another victim of the crimes in VA patient care that go unpunished because of a self-policing bureaucracy that is unpredictable, uneven and unjust, more likely to protect the offender than those harmed.

Take this veteran, Eric, for instance. Each Veterans Affairs facility has its own police force. When something goes wrong, an officer fills out a report, which is sent to the VA Office of the Inspector General.

But the IG does not investigate every complaint they receive. How can that be? How can a police report go un-investigated? Money. The IG staff is not sufficiently staffed to review everything.

You can see where this is headed. The VA police officer must carefully document and interview everyone involved.

But what happens when a VA police officer is called to file out a complaint against a doctor who treats them? Yes, VA

ShutDownTheVA@gmail.com

policers are often veterans themselves and entitled to medical care at VA facilities. Often, these officers can get their medical care at the same facility where they are on duty. Yes, it is allowed. If you were a VA police called to write up a doctor who you have an appointment with next week, would you say something negative in a report?

VA police officers collect information in a pocket notebook. Have you ever tried to write down something when someone is emotional? Or talks fast? Do you get every word? And this is when a VA police officer tries to write up a report. Often, they do not. It's their discretion.

The rules are so loose at VA medical facilities that I am surprised there are not more scandals. I suspect the reason we do not hear about more of them is because it is all designed to protect the facility, the doctor and the administrator at the facility.

The veteran is an afterthought. And there is no requirement for the VA to report anything to authorities outside the VA. It's federal property. There rules are different.

Veterans are receiving healthcare while the system they are trusting is actually so vile, that their life is endangered every time they begin an appointment. Actually, they are less safe when they step foot on VA property than when they are on the streets. That's because the VA has no transparency obligation to the outside world or to veterans.

So, when a veteran is wronged or when laws are broken, civil or criminal, his or her fate hangs in the balance based on a

ShutDownTheVA@gmail.com

corrupt system of self-reporting that will not hang itself for anyone.

I did not give you a cheery introduction to Eric's story. I did not intend to. My intent is to continue to hammer away at veterans like this and to emphasize over and over that this mistreatment happens daily in veterans administration facilities across the nation.

My thanks go to the Huffington Post for gathering the facts of Eric's case and making the public aware of this plight.

I Survived The VA: A Veteran Tells His Shocking Story[12]

Reprinted with permission of the Huffington Post. Thank you for taking care of veterans, those who serve to protect you. Please visit their website to say thanks. www.huffpost.com

Note to Readers:
The facts contained within this story represent crimes existing with a health care crisis within the Veterans Administration. Time is crucial to changing this culture of abuse.

Cat del Valle Castellanos, Contributor
08/28/2015 08:17 pm ET **Updated** Aug 28, 2016

---

[12] https://www.huffpost.com/entry/i-survived-the-va-a-veter_b_8044632

ShutDownTheVA@gmail.com

Warning: Graphic descriptions and video. Names and locations have been changed.

The skin around the lesion on his chest disintegrates with each peel of the dressing. Pus oozes from the dime-sized hole. Six more to go. They were once just scratches. Five. The numbing medication doesn't help. Four. His left pectoral is the worst; an abrasion turned rancid, draining into a small puddle. Three. A ruddy lump of calcified tissue protrudes. Two. Another bandage changed, another rip in his tender skin. One.

Dr. Carlson said he was healing yesterday, but this can't be right. Finally, he succumbs, not to the pain, but logic. Eric's wife drives him to the ER. They've been trying to conceive for over a year, but he knows the medication has destroyed that chance: There will never be a child in their rear-view mirror. Stumbling into the ER, Eric holds his broken ribs in place with his hands.

"You're lucky," says the admitting physician presiding over his frail frame, 30 pounds lighter than a few months earlier. "Six more hours and you'd be dead." His wounds have become septic, his system immunosuppressed far too long.

He wonders if the health care his country promised him is going to kill him. This is not the war Eric signed up to fight. There was red tape from the beginning. Within weeks of arriving in Bosnia in 2001, Eric develops rashes and hives. Doctors attribute the mild episodes to the change in climate and seasonal allergies. They continue for over a year. Soon, Eric develops an umbilical hernia.

ShutDownTheVA@gmail.com

Despite the pain, his sergeant recommends postponing treatment. Eric agrees. Reporting his injury would mean medical holdover status placement; remaining on active duty until he is treated, stabilized, released to duty, or discharged. This also means that instead of returning to his civilian job, he could be stuck behind a desk, pushing papers for up to a year.

Finally, back stateside in 2003, Eric is scheduled for his first surgery. The hernia soon reappears. They try again the next year, this time at another hospital. This surgery, too, is unsuccessful. The implanted Kevlar mesh detaches, leaving him in excruciating pain.

Deprived of targeted immunosuppressants, he develops pathergy, in which skin becomes hyper reactive to minor trauma. It remains undiagnosed.

Eric's third surgery in 2005 is his final one; but he doesn't heal well. While he doesn't want to leave the army, surgical complications have left him scarred and weak. He's more liability than asset. Medically discharged, Eric joins the ranks of those now dependent on the Veterans Administration.

In order to get the VA to cover his healthcare, Eric applies for disability. It takes two years, but he's finally granted a modest ten percent rating. It's good news. He'll have coverage for his injuries, with just a small co-pay; if he can get an appointment. To the VA, it doesn't matter when he began presenting symptoms: Since his illness it wasn't

ShutDownTheVA@gmail.com

diagnosed during service in Bosnia, it isn't 'service connected,' leaving him another name on a burgeoning waitlist.

In 2010, alarmed by his worsening condition, Eric steps up his own research. His symptoms are varied and strange, but after weeks of reviewing the medical literature, he begins to suspect Behcet's Syndrome; a chronic, progressive and disabling auto-inflammatory disease in which swelling damages blood vessels throughout the body, often leading to sores, swelling of the eyes and, eventually, inflammation of the brain, spinal cord, and digestive system. While rare in the United States, Behcet's is common in Southeast Asia and the Middle East, where US military personnel have been involved in decades of war. Genetics may also contribute: Eric's father and his half-brother, Robert, exhibit similar symptoms. There is no blood test for Behcet's; it can only be diagnosed clinically. In fact, with the average time from onset of symptoms to diagnosis at about ten years, chances are that by the time you're diagnosed, multiple organs will have begun to deteriorate.

Luckily, Eric is not entirely dependent on the VA. He has private health insurance through his work as a defense contractor in DC, enabling him to seek treatment from top neurologists at Georgetown University Hospital. He presents his case, and after a negative workup for other rheumatic diseases, they agree. Shortly after, one of the world's top Behcet's experts at NYU reconfirms what they already know. For Eric, half a world away and nine years after Bosnia, the multi-organ system involvement, family history, and

ShutDownTheVA@gmail.com

environmental factors converge: He's diagnosed with Behcet's.

Soon after, he receives a letter from his battalion physician in Bosnia. Looking back, he misdiagnosed Eric. What he saw were the initial symptoms of Behcet's. While his treatment is just beginning, the progressive illness means chronic absences from his private sector job. Eric is soon terminated, and COBRA coverage runs dry a few months later.

Most private insurance plans don't cover what he needs anyway: an inflammatory response suppressant known as Remicade. Even with the Affordable Care Act, Eric can't find an insurance policy that will pay more than 50% of the bill, rendering the $10,000 dollar a month medication far too expensive. The VA HealthCare System, however, will cover it fully just nine dollars a dose.

By this point, the Behcet's has progressed from his kidneys to his chest, finally taking hold of his brain, producing severe neurological complications including episodic loss of balance and sight disruption, anxiety, and tremors. The muggy DC summers exacerbate his lesions. Eric and his wife decided that come fall, they will move back west. Eric's family is there and the cost of living, cheaper. They need the extra cash for medical bills.

Georgetown places him on high-dose corticosteroids in an effort to prevent permanent brain damage. It's meant to be a temporary measure, a holdover until he can get to VA facility in his hometown, where he'll no doubt be provided

ShutDownTheVA@gmail.com

the intravenous Remicade. Upon arrival, Eric is assigned to the VA healthcare System's Dr. David Carlson, an internist and family practitioner. Eric arrives prepared with the diagnosis from NYU, from Georgetown, the letter from his battalion physician, and a novella's worth of medical records. The lesions, the tests, the expert opinions, the pain; Bosnia itself, are all piled in front of Dr. Carlson. The overloaded doctor, however, refuses to read them.

Soldiers are to be "Army Strong." They have to be to survive. Eric, however, breaks down. He cries, imploring Dr. Carlson to review his history. Georgetown had recommended weaning him off the high dose steroids after a month in order to avoid side effects like osteoporosis, ulcers, and increased susceptibility to infection, the latter of which could have permanent consequences for an already compromised inflammatory patient.

Dr. Carlson tells Eric to "save it for Salt Lake," referring to the city's VA Medical Center, where Eric will be sent to undergo invasive procedures to re-diagnose what has already been confirmed. Eric is frustrated, haggard, and God, the pain. If he wants treatment, however, he'll have to play by VA rules. Only the VA doesn't send him to Salt Lake.

Since his Behcet's isn't "service connected," he has to pay his own way. He's scheduled for five appointments, each in a different week. Explaining that he can't afford ten plane fights, five hotel stays, five rental cars, and roughly twenty meals, the VA acquiesces, arranging a week's worth of invasive and repetitive tests he doesn't need. The tests are scheduled for May, five months later.

ShutDownTheVA@gmail.com

While he waits, Eric can cease the steroids and slowly let the inflammation smother his organs, one by one, in hopes that he'll get the Remicade in time to revive them, or he can continue the steroids and risk not only the side effects but a highly weakened immune system in which case the tiniest infection could turn lethal. It's a simple question with an unknown answer: Which one will kill him first? He chooses to remains on the high-dose corticosteroids, turning the transitory medication into a six-month affair.

Back from Salt Lake, Eric calls Dr. Carlson's office, satisfied that he will finally be weaned from the steroids- and that the doctor will no longer be able to refute the reconfirmed diagnosis. He can't get an appointment in the next week or so, but he's on the waitlist- they'll call at the first opening. It can't be too long; Dr. Carlson requested to see him as soon as he returned.

A week passes, then June turns into July. He calls. August. No movement. September. October. Carlson, it turns out, is on paternity leave. Rather than schedule Eric with another doctor, he sits on what would later be termed a fraudulent waitlist. He remains there, without access to the medications requested by the VA's own doctors to negate the steroids' negative effects.

The visits to the ER grow more frequent as the months of high-dose steroids manifest: He's left with low bone density; border lining on osteoporosis.

November. December. January.

X-ray studies show early onset osteoarthritis of the hips and shoulders. He didn't need to see the x-ray; his joints now ache with the pain and stiffness so commonly associated with arthritis, despite being only 35 years old. His bones have become so brittle that a three-foot stumble dislodges several ribs. Formerly a distance runner, Eric can't walk half a mile without stopping for rest.

February. March. April.

On May 27th, 2014 following a substantial increase in the Remicade dosage, and his lesions now dripping bloody brown liquid, Eric manages to make an emergency appointment with Dr. Carlson. The nurse agrees his wounds have deteriorated; he's prescribed painkillers until his scheduled appointment in two days.

Two days later, a haggard, overwrought Eric walked into Dr. Carlson's office. Carlson tells Eric he must be picking at the lesions on chest. Carlson implies that Eric is mentally ill, a doctor-shopping hypochondriac.

Shaken by Dr. Carlson's advice, Eric documents his experience that afternoon, videoing himself caring for his "healing" wounds. It seems to be the only way to prove he's not suffering from a fictitious illness. He slowly removes the bandages to disturb as little skin as possible but small sections crumble and wounds ooze pus. He's not following Dr. Carlson's directions: He needs a topical numbing agent to get through the pain and an antiseptic only makes logical sense. That night, Eric calls two of his old friends, doctors.

ShutDownTheVA@gmail.com

They haven't seen the wounds yet, but the description is enough to tell Eric to go to the ER immediately.

ER physicians indicate that they do not think he is the source of the symptoms but that they appear "typical of a highly immunosuppressed state." A CT scan confirms the tunneling latent infection throughout his chest wall. He's placed on antibiotics.

"Six more hours and you'd be dead."

The staff is under a communication ban so that Eric can be evaluated without the prejudice of his previous doctors. After a few days, Eric is ready to be discharged, but he knows he won't find private insurance to cover the Remicade. Eric has again found himself in the unimaginable position of only having the VA, the organization whose negligence has nearly killed him, to turn to for help.

In preparation for departure, he contacts the VA to be switched to another clinic nearby, in hopes of finding an objective practitioner. But there's a note in his file. Despite VA policy that patients have freedom of choice in primary care clinics, he's only to see Dr. Carrillo, the director of both clinics, and Dr. Carlson's boss. Even though he's exhausted, Eric holds his ground until a patient service representative finally gives in to VA policy.

Eric is hopeful when he first meets the new doctor, but Dr. Truscott is clearly skeptical. No doubt he's heard about Eric. After reviewing his medical history, Dr. Truscott is no longer suspicious; he's dumbfounded. It's clear what has

ShutDownTheVA@gmail.com

happened to Eric, the records show it. Sure enough, another MRI shows the development of avascular necrosis, the death of bone tissue associated with long-term use of steroids.

Maybe now, maybe this time, maybe outside the VA system, this veteran will get the help his country promised. Eric is lucky, in a way. He'll never fully recover, but he didn't die on the waitlist like thousands of others. But that's just the reason he's telling his story.

Leave no man behind.

A formal complaint to the Office of the Inspector General, whose mission is "to prevent and to detect criminal activity, waste, abuse, and fraud," elicits the following response: "Because we receive more complaints than the OIG has resources to review in depth, we limit investigative efforts to issues that have the most serious potential risk to Veterans and VA operations or for which the OIG is the only forum for relief."
In other words, you're shit out of luck.

After repeated attempts to have claim addressed, he authors a letter to the Medical Chief of Staff of his VA facility, Dr. McDevitt. He's told to contact the center's risk manager, who tells him he has one option: file a civil lawsuit and to have his counsel contact the VA regional counsel office. But that's not actually his only option.

The Code of Federal Regulations designates that the VA has a legal obligation to disclose to the Veteran any harm done by the VA in the course of his or her treatment. He informs them of this.

They'll get back to him.

Dr. McDevitt calls along with the risk manager. They'll write a "disclosure of adverse event" letter. They summarize its contents over the phone, but he'll have to submit a formal records request to obtain a copy. Eric goes back to his initial clinic a few weeks later to obtain a full copy of his records. He talks to the patient privacy advocate, who drops an interesting fact: Early the previous summer, right after Eric's hospitalization, nearly the entire staff in the nursing and scheduling departments had been transferred or promoted to other positions at various locations within the VA system.

Eric asks the nurse to provide a list of who had access or made changes to his medical file. She's confused. Despite VA policy, which denotes that patients that may present a risk of malpractice liability must be marked as private, Eric's records weren't tagged, meaning there's no way to see what changes were made- or what's been redacted.

While the American government is strong, so are the people who have the right and the ability to stand up when strength becomes tyranny. The VA has, in effect, told Eric the same thing it's told thousands of other veterans. File a civil lawsuit, and good luck trying to prove it; a method that's sure to be more difficult in Eric's case, given the VA's ability to rewrite history. There's a reason, however, why nearly 70%

ShutDownTheVA@gmail.com

of all claims against them are eventually granted at some level on appeal. It's easier to throw money out the back door than face the media on the front lawn. But Eric won't be settling. The VA needs change more than he needs the money.

The VA should be the fulfillment of a promise: health care in the service of those way we claim to honor most, those who have worn the uniform and offered the last, full measure of their worth for their nation. It has become, in reality, a vending machine, dispensing care through a maze of impersonal, bureaucratic machinery that is inured to patient needs and soldiers' pain. It is top-down health care, trying to deliver compassion through an ever-more complicated Rube Goldberg machine that tries to cure too much bureaucracy with more bureaucracy, paperwork, and regulation.

What we have today is a VA that is only able to fit patients to whatever health care they are able to give, instead of fitting care to the patient.

The tragedy is not that this is the worst the VA can do for our soldiers. It's that this is the best they can do.

ShutDownTheVA@gmail.com

Question for Readers

Do you know Eric? Do you know the rest of his story?
I would like to make readers aware of new developments in
his case.

Please forward information to me at:
shutdowntheva@gmail.com. Thank you.

VA Medical Malpractice Settlements

ShutDownTheVA@gmail.com

Story #9 [13]

2000 – 2019

Malpractice

Selections reprinted with permission of the lawyersandsettlements.com. Thank you for taking care of veterans, those who serve to protect you. Please visit their website to say thanks. *www.lawyersandsettlements.com*

Let's take a moment to get a better understanding of malpractice and what methods veterans have for compensation when the Veterans Administration does something bad to them.

First, it's important to know that veterans do not have the same legal rights to sue a doctor as a private citizen. This applies when the doctor is a VA employee.

---

[13]https://www.lawyersandsettlements.com/lawsuit/veteran_medical_malpractice.html

Second, it's important to know veterans have zero legal rights to sue a doctor who harms them at the VA when that doctor is a VA contractor.

And active duty military have no legal rights to file lawsuits either.

It's a crock, right? But consider this: they are suing you, the taxpayer, when a claim is filed. That's because you are the government, or at least that's the legal concept called sovereign immunity that protects the federal government from most legal liability. In other words, you cannot sue yourself.

But this is not a discussion of sovereign immunity. This is a discussion about the lack of due process available to military and veterans. Quite ironic isn't it? Defenders of our freedoms don't have constitutional rights to due process? But it's true.

So how much in malpractice settlements are paid at the VA compared to the world of the private citizen?

Here's some examples[14] of veterans wronged by the VA. The "settlement" amounts shown are for damages filed under the Federal Tort Claims Act, the method veterans must use to seek malpractice compensation.

---

[14]https://www.lawyersandsettlements.com/lawsuit/veteran_medical_malpractice.html

ShutDownTheVA@gmail.com

- Four veterans died due to medical malpractice at the Coatesville Veterans Affairs Medical Clinic, leading to $1.4 million in settlements with the VA, according to The Center for Investigative Reporting. Four families filed _wrongful death_ lawsuits against the VA that included:
    o Failure to monitor a patient; filed on June 26, 2003 and closed on Jan. 1, 2005 for $100,000.
    o The improper management of a psychiatric patient; filed on Oct. 3, 2005, and closed on Feb. 2, 2008, for $495,578.
    o A wrongful diagnosis or misdiagnosis of a patient; filed on April 16, 2010, and closed on Aug. 19, 2011, for $300,000.
    o Failure to monitor a patient; filed on April 23, 2010, and closed on Dec. 1, 2011, for $500,000. Clerks at the Fort Collins VA clinic were shown how to falsify appointment records so it appeared that doctors were seeing patients within the agency' goal period, according to USA Today. (The VA' official policy is that patients should be able to see a medical professional within 14 days of their request or preferred appointment date. If the patient must wait longer, the delay should be documented.)

Now, here is what lawyersandsettlements.com has to say about the impact to the taxpayer from malpractice claims at the VA[15]:

---

[15]https://www.lawyersandsettlements.com/lawsuit/veteran_medical_malpractice.html

ShutDownTheVA@gmail.com

- VA records showed that malpractice payments increased 28 percent in 2012 from 2011.
- The US Treasury' Judgment Fund paid out $72 million in 2011.
- Taxpayers have spent at least $700 million to resolve claims filed against the veteran's agency since 2001.
- As of May 2014, the VA has settled 68 federal trial court cases brought in 42 venues, from Maine to Southern California. Five of those settlements stemmed from the Northern District of Georgia and the Atlanta VA Medical Center, which supplies coverage for 130,000 veterans. (B.N. Veterans can take a malpractice claim to civil court if the VA denies responsibility and doesn't pay out.)
- The four Veterans Affairs Medical Centers in North Carolina settled 29 wrongful death cases worth $4.75 million in the decade after the Sept. 11 attacks.
- In Illinois, 25 deaths at the Marion VA resulted in $7.7 million in wrongful death settlements, according to the *Chicago Tribune* April 30, 2014).
- The Tribune also reported wrongful death payments to the survivors of 12 veterans who died under the care of the agency's three Chicago-area hospitals, including $300,000 to the family of a veteran who died at the Jesse Brown VA Medical Center.
- In a wrongful-death settlement against the Fayetteville VA facility, the agency paid out $750,000. The death was caused by the VA' "failure to diagnose,"meaning a conclusion that the patient had no disease or condition.
- Tracy Eiswert' husband and Iraq War veteran Scott Eiswert, age 31, shot himself in the head in 2008.

ShutDownTheVA@gmail.com

- o The Nashville, Tenn., VA had denied his disability claim for PTSD.
- o Three months after his death the agency admitted it made an error and began sending Tracy Eiswert survivor benefits checks of $1,195 a month.
- o After Scott' suicide, she moved into her car with her two young children. She has now filed a wrongful death lawsuit against the VA, mainly due to the toll her husband's suicide took on their children.
- o The case, filed in 2010, is still pending.
- A veteran at the Phoenix VA was diagnosed with reflux, although his blood pressure was high. A VA doctor recommended a cardiac stress test but he had to wait seven weeks. He died of a heart attack a few days later. The case settled for $800,000 in May, 2014.
- In 2007 Christopher Ellison went to a Philadelphia VA medical center in Philadelphia to get eight teeth extracted.
  - o The surgery left him permanently incapacitated.
  - o Ellison and his family received $17.5 million in a malpractice judgment against the Department of VA.
- Veterans Affairs wrongful death cases from Sept. 11, 2001, to Nov. 4, 2011:
  - o Families who received payments. 978
  - o Millions of dollars paid to these families. $209.7
  - o Median payment in these claims. $150,000
  - o Median number of days to process each claim. 673

Disclaimer: LawyersandSettlements.com claim that their data was obtained and analyzed by The Center for Investigative Reporting.

ShutDownTheVA@gmail.com

Read More at LawyersandSettlements.com

Lubin & Meyer PC

Now, let's look at what one law firm, Lubin & Meyer PC, claims are some, not all, of the settlement amounts they have negotiated for their clients over the years.[16] This is a partial list according to the firm. Why is this important to know? Because it shows how screwed veterans are when they are harmed by doctors at the Veterans Administration.

Veterans occasionally get a reasonable settlement, as we showed previously. But in most cases, a veterans' claims are denied. And when a veteran's case is settled, the payout for harm, for damage to their body that sometimes kills or cripples them for life, is a pittance compared to what a private citizen negotiates in malpractice cases.

Here's the Lubin & Meyer partial list of settlements in the world of private sector care, broken down by type. Pay particular attention to the amounts and type of claim.

Heart Attack / Stroke / Cardiac / Aneurysm

- **$11.5 million verdict -** Cardiac arrest, neurological injuries in 18-month-old girl

- **$5.8 million verdict -** Jury finds physician negligent in heart attack death

---

[16]http://www.lubinandmeyer.com/cases/caselist.html#personalinjury

ShutDownTheVA@gmail.com

- **$5.8 million verdict** - Heart attack death trial report
- **$5 million** - Misdiagnosed cardiac arrest causing brain injury
- **$4.75 million** - Failure to respond to elevated Troponin results in heart attack
- **$4 million** - Aortic dissection diagnosis delay leads to paralysis
- **$3.75 million** - Failure to properly treat atrial fibrillation leads to massive stroke
- **$3 million** - Cardiac arrest resulting in anoxic brain injury
- **$2.9 million** - Stroke malpractice mediation results in settlement
- **$2 million** - Cardiac arrhythmia wrongful death settlement
- **$1.74 million** - Cardiologist and PCP failure to diagnose and treat chest pains
- **$1.5 million** - Emergency department aortic dissection death
- **$1.4 million** - Settlement in pulmonary embolus death
- **$1.25 million** - Aortic aneurysm wrongful death lawsuit
- **$1.1 million** - Failure to recognize EKG changes leads to myocardial infarction death
- **$1 million** - Unnecessary heart bypass surgery lawsuit settles
- **$1 million** - TIA stroke lawsuit settles
- **$1 million** - EMT malpractice heart attack (UMass Memorial EMS, Worcester)
- **$1 million** - Heart attack malpractice settlement
- **$1 million** - Settlement in heart attack death
- **$850,000** - Cardiac monitor alarm fatigue lawsuit at MGH settles
- **$750,000** - Doc pays in heart attack malpractice case: Failure to diagnose and treat

Misdiagnosis of Cancer / Failure to Diagnose Treat Cancer

ShutDownTheVA@gmail.com

- **$19.8 million verdict -** Cervical cancer malpractice case
- **$16.7 million verdict -** Lung cancer lawsuit; radiologist misread x-ray
- **$11.3 million verdict -** IVF doctor failure to diagnose ovarian cancer
- **$11 million verdict -** Breast cancer wrongful death award
- **$6.8 million judgment -** Kidney cancer diagnosis delay by Lowell General doc
- **$5 million -** Settlement for delay in diagnosis of chordoma cancer
- **$4.5 million -** Settlement for delay in diagnosis of colorectal cancer
- **$4.5 million verdict -** Breast cancer diagnosis delay
- **$4.25 million settlement -** Cancer diagnosis delay in NH
- **$3.5 million -** Liver cancer diagnosis delay
- **$2.84 million verdict -** Failure to screen for prostate cancer
- **$2.5 million -** Pathologist failed to identify cancer in appendix and record it
- **$2.5 million -** Metastatic liver cancer diagnosis delay
- **$2.5 million verdict -** Misdiagnosed breast cancer
- **$2.06 million verdict -** Bowel obstruction wrongful death lawsuit
- **$2 million -** Failure to treat melanoma
- **$2 million -** PSA test results withheld— prostate cancer diagnosis delay
- **$2 million -** Failure to diagnose colon cancer leads to premature death
- **$1.9 million -** Lung cancer lawsuit involving Boston Medical Center radiologist
- **$1.8 million -** Failure to diagnose and treat lung cancer
- **$1.75 million -** Delay in diagnosis of esophageal cancer
- **$1.75 million -** Delay in diagnosis of thyroid cancer
- **$1.75 million -** Delay in diagnosis of metastatic breast cancer
- **$1.6 million verdict -** Medical mistake at Dana Farber re: IV contrast

- **$1.5 million** - Kidney cancer malpractice settlement
- **$1.5 million** - Delay in lung cancer diagnosis; failure to order chest x-ray
- **$1.5 million** - Delay in diagnosis of colon cancer
- **$1.5 million** - Endometrial cancer death lawsuit
- **$1.35 million** - Biopsy delay causes delay in diagnosis of breast cancer
- **$1.25 million** - Delay in diagnosis of leiomyosarcoma
- **$1.25 million** - Failure to diagnose breast cancer
- **$1.25 million** - Delay in diagnosis of lung cancer caused by misread x-ray
- **$1.2 million** - Lung cancer diagnosis delay
- **$1.2 million** - Delay in diagnosis of NH woman's cauda equina syndrome
- **$1 million** - PCP's failure to follow up on abnormal Pap smear causes delay in diagnosis of cervical cancer
- **$1 million** - Failure to follow up on prostate cancer screening
- **$1 million** - Lung cancer claim settles prior to filing of lawsuit
- **$1 million** - Delay in diagnosis of anal cancer
- **$1 million** - Cervical cancer diagnosis delay
- **$1 million** - Pancreatic cancer diagnosis delay; misread CT scan
- **$1 million** - Thyroid cancer diagnosis delay
- **$1 million** - Failure to monitor for liver cancer in Asian man with history of Hepatitis B
- **$1 million** - Failure to diagnose lung cancer
- **$1 million** - Skin cancer (malignent melanoma) death settlement
- **$1 million** - Failure to diagnose rectal cancer
- **$1 million** - Delay in diagnosis of cervical cancer; misread PAP smear
- **$1 million** - Delay in diagnosis of malignant melanoma settlement
- **$1 million** - Delay in diagnosis of colo-rectal cancer

ShutDownTheVA@gmail.com

- **$1 million** - Man dies during a prostatectomy following <u>misdiagnosed prostate cancer</u>
- **$1 million** - Delay in diagnosis of <u>breast cancer</u>
- **$1 million** - <u>Failure to diagnose colon cancer</u> lawsuit
- **$1 million** - <u>Failure to screen for colon cancer</u> malpractice
- **$1 million** - <u>Prostate cancer</u> diagnosis delay
- **$975,000** - <u>Colon cancer delay</u> lawsuit settles pre-trial
- **$900,000** - <u>Radiologists</u> failed to communicate findings in lung cancer lawsuit
- **$900,000** - Delay in diagnosis of <u>thyroid cancer</u> settlement
- **$825,000** - <u>Prostate cancer</u> malpractice settlement
- **$750,000** - <u>Endometrial cancer</u> malpractice lawsuit
- **$500,000** - <u>Testicular cancer</u> malpractice lawsuit
- **$500,000** - <u>Colon cancer</u> wrongful death settlement
- **$450,000** - <u>Breast cancer diagnosis delay</u> settlement

Medical Error, Surgical Error, Medication Error, Misdiagnosis, Medical Negligence

- **$14.5 million verdict** - Jury award to family of woman who died after <u>thyroid surgery</u>
- **$14.5 million verdict** - Brockton surgeon negligent in death during <u>elective thyroid surgery</u>
- **$13.587 million verdict** - Dana-Farber <u>infection death</u> trial finds two docs negligent (trial report)
- **$13.5 million verdict** - $13.5 awarded in <u>Dana-Farber infection</u> death (news article)
- **$13 million verdict** - Widow awarded in husband's post <u>tonsillectomy death</u>
- **$10.7 million verdict** - <u>Post-surgical infection,</u> retained sponge, additional surgeries
- **$7.5 million** - <u>Lab error</u> in stem cell transplant

ShutDownTheVA@gmail.com

- blamed for death of 5-year-old twin
- **$6.8 million** - Woman dies after hiatal hernia surgery Winchester Hospital doc
- **$5.5 million** - Fallon HMO settles in brain infection lawsuit
- **$5.1 million** - Spinal surgery error ends Bobby Jenks' baseball career
- **$4.5 million** - Newton Wellesley Hospital docs agree to pay in girl's death
- **$4.1 million** - Docs lose medical lawsuit in hospital death
- **$4 million** - Failure to monitor blood sugar results in hypoglycemic event
- **$3.75 million** - Paralysis following spinal hematoma
- **$3.5 million** - Death from bowel perforation after disc surgery
- **$3.5 million verdict** - ER delay leads to death of 12-year-old boy
- **$3.5 million verdict** - Breast reduction surgery malpractice case
- **$3.5 million** - Wrongful death settlement involved CT scan
- **$3.5 million** - Settlement for negligence in back surgery
- **$3.2 million verdict** - Misdiagnosis results in lost testicle
- **$3 million** - Anesthesia aspiration death due to undiagnosed bowel obstruction
- **$3 million** - Spinal cord injury from epidural abscess
- **$3 million** - Hospital infection resulting in brain injury
- **$3 million** - Misread CT scan leads to death
- **$2.5 million** - Encephalomyelitis wrongful death lawsuit
- **$2.5 million verdict** - Women's death after surgery to remove ovarian cysts
- **$2.45 million** - Anoxic brain injury of 8-month-old girl
- **$2.25 million** - Delay in spinal surgery
- **$2.2 million** - Surgery error involving epidural

ShutDownTheVA@gmail.com

placement resulting in paraplegia

- **$2 million** - Perforated bowel infection during weight loss surgery
- **$2 million** - Failure to monitor in brain hemorrhage lawsuit settlement
- **$2 million** - Anesthesia death following elective hernia surgery
- **$2 million** - Spinal cord surgery malpractice settlement
- **$2 million** - Negligence in bowel obstruction at Lowell General ER
- **$1.995 million** - Botched spinal surgery results in quadriplegia
- **$1.9 million** - Misinterpreted MRI leads to brain bleed and death
- **$1.85 million** - Doc admits medication error
- **$1.75 million** - Failure to diagnose and treat pulmonary abscess
- **$1.75 million** - Heart surgery malpractice settlement
- **$1.75 million verdict** - New Hampshire man blinded in ER error

- **$1.75 million verdict** - Death after gallbladder surgery at Beth Israel
- **$1.576 million verdict** - Intubation death caused by negligence
- **$1.5 million** - Failure to diagnose perforated intestine
- **$1.5 million** - Surgical error causes facial droop
- **$1.5 million** - Delay of spinal cord surgery results in paraplegia
- **$1.5 million** - Bowel necrosis leads to death and settlement
- **$1.365 million verdict** - Delay of surgery in bowel aspiration death
- **$1.29 million verdict** - Negligence in eye surgery leaves man blind in one eye
- **$1.25 million verdict** - Gallbladder surgery error causes Cape Cod woman injuries requiring reconstructive surgery and long recovery
- **$1.25 million** - Preventable medication error (30x dose of anticoagulant)
- **$1.25 million** - Kidney transplant lawsuit

ShutDownTheVA@gmail.com

- **$1.2 million** - Bacterial infection death lawsuit
- **$1.15 million** - Cataract surgery resulting in blindness in 69-year-old woman
- **$1.15 million** - Cataract surgery error results in vision loss in 56-year-old man
- **$1 million** - NH woman injuried from compartment syndrome following surgery
- **$1 million** - Sinus surgery results in loss of vision (lamina papyracea)
- **$1 million** - Misread CT scan wrongful death lawsuit
- **$1 million** - Negligence in sinus surgery lawsuit
- **$1 million** - Gallbladder surgical error lawsuit settles
- **$1 million** - EMT negligence lawsuit
- **$1 million** - Delay in diagnosis of cauda equina syndrome
- **$1 million** - Delay of spinal surgery - cauda equina lawsuit
- **$1 million** - Mass. General Hospital medication error death
- **$1 million** - Botched gastric bypass dialation
- **$1 million** - Woman's death due to abdominal bleed
- **$1 million** - Diabetes mellitus malpractice claim
- **$1 million** - Medical malpractice involving leg amputation
- **$1 million** - Amitriptyline toxicity death
- **$1 million** - Lithium toxicity brings wrongful death settlement
- **$1 million** - Blindness in one eye
- **$900,000** - Delay in treatment of diabetic ulcer
- **$868,828 verdict** - Surgical mistake during gallbladder surgey
- **$850,000** - Cauda equina diagnosis delay causes permanent injuries
- **$750,000** - Improperly placed feeding tube/sepsis
- **$280,000 verdict** - Jury award for surgical tool left in abdomen

ShutDownTheVA@gmail.com

Catastrophic Personal Injury / Wrongful Death

- **$8.5 million verdict** - Jury awards NH family in wrongful death action against trucking company
- **$6.1 million settlement** - Rhode Island man hit and killed by drunk driver after visiting 5 bars.
- **$6.1 million verdict** - Man killed stadium crash (news coverage 1)
- **$6.1 million verdict** - Man killed in stadium
- fatality (news coverage 2)
- **$3 million** - Death of 23-year-old mentally ill patient at Bridgewater State Hospital
- **$1.73 million** - Climbing wall death
- **$1.25 million** - Auto accident injury lawsuit
- **$1 million** - Hunting accident settlement
- **$1 million** - Forklift accident settlement

Sexual Abuse

- **$8.4 million verdict** - Sex abuse case
- **$1 million** - Psych doc agrees to settlement
- **$750,000** - Psychiatrist pays for violating patient boundaries

Boggles the mind, huh?

How many of these settlements did Lubin & Meyer win against the Veterans Administration for a veteran malpractice claim?

I called Lubin & Meyer and spoke with their PR department, posing this question. The answer: I don't know. A promise to call me back never happened.

Searching the internet, I found no cases where Lubin & Meyer represented a veteran in a case against the Veterans Administration and settled in the veterans' favor.

I don't blame Lubin & Meyer for this. They have a business to run. And suing the government is not a profitable business. Like most law firms, they do not work on veteran's malpractice claims. There's no money in it.

What kinds of settlement amounts do veterans get?
Ok, so here's the good news.

The number of legal settlements made by the Department of Veterans Affairs has more than tripled over the past five years largely due to a spike in medical malpractice cases and bungled construction projects, the Daily News has learned.

The yearly total payments skyrocketed to $338 million in 2015 from $98 million in 2011, according to Treasury Department data obtained via a Freedom of Information Act request.[17]

Now, the bad news. When you read this quote from the VA's 2015 financial report you would think veterans are rolling in dough from malpractice claim settlements.

VA recorded a liability for pending legal claims that are estimated to be paid by the Judgment Fund. This liability is established for all pending claims whether reimbursement

---

[17] https://www.nydailynews.com/news/national/legal-settlements-veterans-affairs-triple-article-1.2654179

is required or not and was $2 billion for 2015 and $1.69 billion for 2014.[18]

Veterans are getting $3.69 billion dollars as settlements in 2014-2015! That's terrific. Not so fast. Read further down the report:

In 2014, the range of exposure was $245 million to $1.3 billion, from 27 cases, of which <u>$93 million was probable and recorded as a liability</u>.

In other words, the chance of veterans getting well over a billion dollars in settlements is slim to none. The payout is more likely to be $93 million in 2014.

Go back to the Lubin & Meyer partial list of settlements for private citizens and pick out $93 million dollars' worth of settlements. And this is one law firm and only a partial list.

$93 million is not chump-change. But consider this:

18

https://www.google.com/url?sa=t&rct=j&q=&esrc=s&source=web&cd=12&ved=2ahUKEwiE7KeOsJXmAhVIwlkKHbEjDy4QFjALegQIAhAC&url=https%3A%2F%2Fwww.va.gov%2Foig%2Fpubs%2FVAOIG-15-01708-36.pdf&usg=AOvVaw0zv36I1tBzd7pNKCUPZD-g

> "Between July 1, 2014 and June 30, 2015, a total
> of 738,212 of these Veterans accessed VA health care"[19]

In other words, the private sector is getting far more lucrative payouts – some say fairer – than veterans are getting for malpractice claims at the Veterans Administration.

Too litigious?

My argument is not about America being an overly litigious nation. Sure, we sue each other, and the payouts can be big

What I am arguing for is a fairer system for veterans, let's say the one they are guaranteed by the constitution they protect by serving in the military.

This is about giving veterans back their rights to due process, when the VA doctors harm them. That's all. Veterans don't deserve something more than private citizens, but they sure deserve the same.

This is why I support privatization of the Veterans Administration. Once veteran's healthcare is out of the purview of the federal government, veterans will be on a level legal playing ground, which they deserve.

Lubin & Meyer PC. They are a good legal firm. Maybe they'll help a few veterans as well.

---

[19]

https://www.publichealth.va.gov/epidemiology/reports/oefo ifond/health-care-utilization/

http://www.lubinandmeyer.com/cases/caselist.html#person alinjury

Read More at LawyersandSettlements.com and

www.lubinandmeyer.com

ShutDownTheVA@gmail.com

Story #10

2013

"They Set Me on Fire"[20]

I am grateful to lawyersandsettlements.com for permission to reprint this article. Thank you for bringing awareness to veterans' issues. www.lawyersandsettlements.com

August 31, 2013

Stafford, WV (West Virginia) American military vet Steven Anthony was already living a life compromised by *Post Traumatic Stress Disorder (PTSD)* when he was suffered another blow to his already fragile mind at a Veteran's hospital in Martinsburg, Virginia. Steven became a victim of *veteran medical malpractice*.

Several months ago, Anthony was admitted for some routine surgery. The plan was to give Anthony a general anesthetic

---

[20] https://www.lawyersandsettlements.com/legal-news/veteran_medical_malpractice/interview-va-hospital-malpractice-medical-19046.html

for knee surgery, and while he was in the operating room, remove a lesion on his forehead.

"As I lay on the operating table, my mind was telling me I was getting hot. I woke up to see flames all around me," says Anthony.
"I reached up and pulled fire from my face."

The operating room team had been using an electric cauterizing device to control bleeding during the removal of the lesion. It ignited Anthony's oxygen supply and caused the cotton gauze around his face to catch fire.

"Everyone else backed off and Steven burnt his hands as he tore the burning material from his face," says his attorney Anthony Williams, who is a former marine and judge advocate, and has represented members of the military on a variety of issues. "He suffered some superficial burns on his face and hands but the real issue aggravated his PTSD."

Already an individual with significant "social issues" and diagnosed with PTSD long ago after a tour in the military in the mid-80s, the operating room flame event seemed to send Anthony reeling further out of the main stream. A few months after the incident at the VA hospital, Steven Anthony tried to commit suicide and found himself back in the hospital.

The hospital offered Anthony consideration in the amount of $30,000. When he refused that, the hospital offered $40,000. He's now suing for $1.3 million in Federal District Court in Martinsburg, West Virginia.

"They are making me sue them for this instead of paying the claim," Anthony told LAS. "They could give a damn about me having to deal with this on a daily basis and that aggravates me to no end, which in turn causes my PTSD to go off the charts."

"Who is to say whether it is worth $1.3 million or $3.1 million?," says his lawyer William Anthony. "Something in his psyche is really scrambled. I don't think liability is at issue here. The only question is how much is it worth and that will be up to the magistrate," says Williams.

"He has a serious lack of trust now with the VA. These are his caregivers," says Williams who served 20 years in the military.

"I don't want to say anything bad about the VA. There are plenty of people doing that nowadays. I think the VA is taking steps to improve services, especially with the ever-increasing number of service members who are having problems," says Williams. "But as for this one veteran, their efforts are falling far short."

Anthony Williams is the founding partner at Anthony Williams and Associates in Stafford, West Virginia, and a graduate of DePaul University College of Law. A former marine, Williams served as a judge advocate with the US Military. With over 20 years of legal experience, Attorney Williams has successfully handled complex civil and criminal matters in state and federal courts. He now practices in the areas of Family Law; Divorce; Child

ShutDownTheVA@gmail.com

Custody and Support; Criminal Defense, including Court-Martials and Appeals; and Civil Litigation, including Personal Injury and Medical Malpractice.

https://www.lawyersandsettlements.com/lawsuit/veteran_medical_malpractice.html

Read More at LawyersandSettlements.com
Read more stories by Brenda Craig

ShutDownTheVA@gmail.com

Story #11

2011

VA Medical Malpractice: Veteran Cries Discrimination[21]

April 5, 2011, 8:00AM. By Jane Mundy

Portland, OR

Not only does Arthur believe that his VA doctor is guilty of *VA medical malpractice* after a botched surgery, he also accuses the VA hospital (and the federal government) of discriminating against Korean and Vietnam veterans.

"It all started several years ago when I had micro-surgery to treat a Hiatal hernia," says Arthur. (This type of hernia is a condition in which a part of the stomach protrudes upward into the chest, through an opening in the diaphragm.) The VA doctors told Arthur that they could stop his acid reflux problem by micro-surgery that involved removing a piece of

---

[21] https://www.lawyersandsettlements.com/legal-news/veteran_medical_malpractice/interview-va-hospital-malpractice-veterans-medical-2-16402.html

ShutDownTheVA@gmail.com

his stomach and making another esophagus. "But during surgery, they accidentally cut a nerve on the side of my stomach that produces the acid that starts the digestion process; they also lost a needle in my stomach during surgery."

According to Arthur, he was the first person to undergo this kind of microsurgery procedure at the VA hospital up on the hill in Portland. "I think I was a guinea pig and they didn't tell me about their mistakes until I had the big surgery—the second one," he explains.

"A few months after the surgery I was getting swollen and very sick. I had more x-rays, including one where you eat _radiated scrambled eggs_ and they watch it digest. Well it didn't digest and that meant another surgery. This time they took out a chunk of food the size of a softball, and opened up the bottom flap of my stomach, so I digested straight into my bowel from then on. And I still am.

"The doctor came into my room a few days after this second surgery and explained what happened and why it was necessary—because of the mistakes that happened during the first surgery. I don't think they knew the nerve had been cut until I was in the operating room—the only thing they were certain of was the lost needle, which he told me not to worry about because I would digest it in my bowels. It sounds crazy but this is all documented in my medical records.

"And now I have another problem: I just had yet another surgery to stretch my esophagus because I was having a hard

ShutDownTheVA@gmail.com

time swallowing. They scoped me during that surgery and accidentally cut a nerve that controls the stomach, bowel, small and large intestine that moves the food along. Now, none of the signals are reaching the stomach etc. to move the digestion along.

"The doctor told me—and my girlfriend was there so she can back up this statement—that I was "plain f**ked." I have lost over 50 lbs in the last few months. I can barely eat, I can't do anything. And now my doctor is avoiding me so I don't know what to do.

"Naturally I have to be very careful about my diet, but no matter how careful, I go through 'serious dump syndrome': When I go to the bathroom it hurts so much that I literally black out sometimes. In the last 45 days I have been to ER twice at the VA hospital because of this problem. Unfortunately, I have no choice: because I'm a disabled veteran I have to go to the VA hospital.

"Last Wednesday I had the radiated egg x-ray again and still haven't got the results. I'm sitting here wondering what the heck I'm supposed to do next; I'm just getting sicker and weaker. I haven't even had an apology, which is no surprise. "I even had problems getting my meds for acid reflux, stomach cramps and bloating, and pain meds from the nerve damage. My prescriptions are sent by mail because I am housebound but sometimes they are days late. And I only get to see my doctor about once a year—that's the way they treat veterans.

"When I returned from Vietnam, I used to get really good

care. I was injured over there and suffered very bad back problems so I collected disability benefits. The nurses were really good to everyone. But now that we have all the new vets coming back from overseas, they are being more sensationalized—they are taken care of first. The Korean and Vietnam vets are set aside while the new guys get special treatment—that's the way I see it anyway. I am a typical example of someone being discriminated against.

"I would like to find out what I can do about my condition because I know it is wrong: someone has to stand up sooner or later…"

Read More at LawyersandSettlements.com

Read more stories by Jane Mundy

ShutDownTheVA@gmail.com

Cancer

ShutDownTheVA@gmail.com

Even the Veterans Administration admits misdiagnosis of illness happens in the United States. To set the stage for this section on cancer, I want to present this story first.

Story #12

2014

Twelve million patients misdiagnosed yearly in America, says VA researcher [22]

July 18, 2014
Dr. Hardeep Singh of VA's Houston-based Center for Innovations in Quality, Effectiveness and Safety studies issues relating to patient safety and the electronic medical record.

In business or the military, leaders improve by studying the results of their efforts for lessons learned. In medicine though, the same feedback loops don't always exist. "Right now providers often diagnose and treat patients in an open loop fashion," says Dr. Hardeep Singh, chief of health policy,

---

[22]

https://www.research.va.gov/currents/summer2014/summer2014-8.cfm

quality, and informatics at the VA Center for Innovations in Quality, Effectiveness and Safety, at the Houston VA Medical Center. "They think their patients are getting better but there is no tracking system...no feedback loop to find out what's happening. In many of these cases, no news isn't necessarily good news."

Singh recently authored a study, published online May 5 in the journal *BMJ Quality & Safety*, which estimated about five percent of outpatient diagnoses are erroneous. "In layman's terms, it's a misdiagnosis," says Singh, also an associate professor at Baylor College of Medicine. "Say you come in complaining of left leg pain and swelling and I think you have arthritis, and then three days later it turns out you had a blood clot.

Estimate based on three past studies

For the study, Singh analyzed the results of three previous studies, based in VA and in private systems with electronic medical records. Two of the studies used algorithms to detect certain high-risk situations suggestive of error and the third examined patients with lung cancer. Singh's team then compared those results to the U.S. adult population. Based on the results, Singh estimates the nationwide misdiagnosis rate at 5.08 percent, or around 12 million U.S. patients per year.

Those errors can not only affect a patient's health, but also have a financial impact.

ShutDownTheVA@gmail.com

"Take for example the patient with the clot in his leg," says Singh. "If that clot later travels to his lung and he has to be hospitalized for 10 days, we are adding financial cost t
o the psychological and health-related impact of that error." VA, for its part, has more knowledge of what happens to its patients because it's a closed system. "We've got more measurable data in VA," says Singh. "If a VA provider sends the patient to a specialist, the provider will know the result of that specialist visit soon after it's completed. VA maintains comprehensive electronic records of outpatient and inpatient events and provides a far better look on patient care events. That's not always the case outside of VA, where providers might not receive updates from other providers."

'Lots of data and not enough time'

Nevertheless, even with VA's electronic medical record, errors do occur, says Singh, whose March 2010 study in _The American Journal of Medicine_ found errors in follow-up of abnormal lab results despite VA's EMR. "It [EMR] is a very good system, but there is a lot of information there and providers are very busy and sometimes miss things," says Singh. "Lots of data and not enough time can mean information chaos."

In an editorial in the _Journal of General Internal Medicine_ in May 2014, Singh commented that just because most patients don't contact their clinicians to let them know they are not better, doctors should not assume that no news from the patient is good news. "Receiving routine feedback on patient outcomes could help physicians recalibrate their confidence in diagnostic and treatment decisions," he wrote.

ShutDownTheVA@gmail.com

"Processes to provide clinicians with constructive feedback need to be developed. Further research is also needed to study how clinicians deal with diagnostic uncertainty and how that uncertainty is best communicated to patients," says Singh.

Meanwhile, Singh says patients should ensure they're sharing information with their providers and should feel empowered to contact them. "If you get a test, you must follow up. Reach back to the doctor and don't assume things are normal," he says. Doctors too, need to find time in their schedules to seek feedback. "It's a cultural shift. Right now we don't get any feedback, so we assume everything we do is correct and that patients are getting better. We need better follow-up systems and need to track patients better so we can prevent them from 'falling through the cracks' of the health system."

Story #13

2018

In the previous story we discovered that diagnosing illness is difficult and sometimes mistakes are made. I can understand that these things happen. Doctors are only human even though VA nurses often refer to them as "ego cases."

Dr. Singh says 12 million people are mis-diagnosed annually. To be honest, as high trained as doctors are supposed to be, that seems like a very high – too high – level of mistakes.

According to *Managed Care* magazine,

"...Misdiagnosis causes 80,000 deaths a year, by some counts."[23]

---

[23]

https://www.managedcaremag.com/archives/2019/3/doing-harm-american-health-care-case-misdiagnosis

That is an astounding number! And those are the deaths. What about the patients that are still alive? What consequences are they suffering because of this, is it too harsh to say, incompetence?

The Veterans Administration will not release numbers on the number of patients in their system that are mis-diagnosed or for whom that misdiagnosis caused death or injury.

Why? Well, the level is extraordinarily higher than in the civilian population. I also imagine that the VA simply does not have effective ways to measure all the mistakes it makes.

What could be worse than to be told you have a bad back only to discover you have cancer? Other than dying, I cannot think of anything worse than that.

One of the best investigative reporters in the country is Steve Andrews at WFLA-TV in Tampa, Florida. Here is the story I just mentioned, and Steve is the one who reported it.

Family of cancer-stricken veteran wants answers from the VA after misdiagnosis[24]

Investigations by: Steve Andrews
Posted: Mar 2, 2018 / 01:40 PM EST / Updated: Mar 2, 2018 / 01:40 PM EST

---

[24] https://www.wfla.com/8-on-your-side/investigations/family-of-cancer-stricken-veteran-wants-answers-from-the-va-after-misdiagnosis/

ShutDownTheVA@gmail.com

PINELLAS COUNTY, Fla. (WFLA) – The agony of cancer continues to take its toll on a Pasco County veteran and his family.

The family of Navy veteran Lonnie Kilpatrick is searching for answers after they say the VA at Bay Pines missed stage 4 cancer that's spread to most of his organs and bones.

"It's heartbreaking when you see him in there crying and throwing up and he says, Why does it have to be cancer?" said Lonnie's wife Sheila Kilpatrick.

After our investigation into the deadly misdiagnosis aired, the hospital's Chief of Staff Dr. Dominique Thuriere said she plans to open a peer review of this case.

Dr. Thuriere wants to know if any treatment opportunities for Kilpatrick were missed.

Records show the hospital diagnosed and treated Lonnie for kidney cancer four years ago. Since that diagnosis, he's experienced worsening hip and back pain. Lonnie was also treated for spinal stenosis and arthritis. The pain grew so intense that in January, his family took him to a civilian hospital.

"They came back in and said he's got cancer, and it's everywhere," explained Lonnie's daughter Keri Ackerson who is a nurse case manager.

ShutDownTheVA@gmail.com

Dr. Thuriere agreed to answer questions about Lonnie's case as long as the family agreed and Lonnie signed a consent form, which he did.

So, how did doctors miss a cancer diagnosis?

"Well the cancer wasn't missed," explained Dr. Thuriere. "Obviously the patient has been treated for a renal cell carcinoma starting in 2013."

Since Lonnie was diagnosed with cancer, the VA has not seen any evidence of re-occurrence, the doctor told me.

But if he had the disease, and he's complaining of back pain, why wasn't anyone at Bay Pines connecting the dots?

"The imaging that we've done with an MRI, MRI'S is superior to CT and they can see all the bone structures in his pelvis and his abdomen and there was no evidence that there were other tumors or there was cancer in his bones," said Dr. Thuriere.

According to the doctor, Lonnie's medical issues are varied and complex and include a heart transplant, cancer, a degenerative spinal condition. She said the VA put a lot of eyes on him.

But with all these eyes on Lonnie, why didn't anyone pick up on the possibility of cancer?

"I think you should entertain the possibility that the cancer was not there at that time," Dr. Thuriere said.

Earlier this week, pain and fatigue overwhelmed Lonnie as he waited at an outside cancer for the VA to approve his treatment.

So, if Lonnie has stage 4 cancer, he lost 50 pounds and he can hardly get out of bed, why is he waiting five hours for VA authorization?

"No, that should not happen," explained Dr. Thuriere. "No one should be expected to suffer or to wait for that if a veteran needs to have his care authorized that is something that is done immediately it's something that we monitor, if there was a delay in that I will look into that as well."

If you have something that you think should be investigated contact the Target 8 Helpline at 1 800 338-0808 or contact Steve Andrews at sandrews@wfla.com.

Story #14

2014

So, while we're in Florida, let's hop across Tampa Bay to St. Petersburg and the Bay Pines VA Hospital to learn of another veteran's cancer misdiagnosis in 2014.

St. Pete veteran dies after VA's delay in cancer diagnosis[25]

Each morning and night, Lillie Lalley, 81, widow of Horace Lalley, kisses photos of him that line their home’s walls. He died of cancer in October 2012.
By Times Staff Writer
Published May 23, 2014

ST. PETERSBURG — Navy veteran Horace J. Lalley suffered urinary tract problems for years with symptoms he

---

[25] https://www.tampabay.com/news/military/veterans/st-pete-veteran-dies-after-vas-delay-in-cancer-diagnosis/2181224/

ShutDownTheVA@gmail.com

regularly reported to doctors at the C.W. Bill Young VA Medical Center.

Blood in his urine. A burning sensation and pain when he went to the bathroom. Frequent urination at night.

The diagnosis again and again: urinary tract infection. But doctors were wrong. In fact, a malignancy was growing in Lalley's bladder.

Lalley's family says the Department of Veterans Affairs hospital missed important clues about Lalley's bladder cancer, including significant bleeding, and failed to order timely radiological scans and other tests that would have led to an accurate diagnosis.

By the time Lalley was referred to a urologist and scans completed by May 2012, it was too late. The veteran had end-stage bladder cancer.

Lalley died on Oct. 23, 2012. He was 76.

Jason Dangel, a spokesman for the Young VA, said Friday that the hospital, formerly known as Bay Pines, was not aware of allegations of improper care in the Lalley case until contacted by the *Tampa Bay Times*. He said facility physicians would conduct a "thorough review" to determine if Lalley's care was deficient.

The VA nationally is under intense scrutiny after reports of preventable deaths due to delayed treatment at VA facilities.

ShutDownTheVA@gmail.com

Some veteran groups and lawmakers have demanded VA Secretary Eric Shinseki resign.

In Tampa Bay, the agency has said there have been no veteran deaths involving a narrow category of cases — patients who were not timely referred to a specialist for gastrointestinal cancers. The VA reports 23 such deaths nationally.

But Lalley's case suggests a wider review in Tampa Bay and around the nation may identify additional deaths that have escaped scrutiny.

"If it happened to my dad, it's probably happened to others," said Lalley's daughter, Denise Voyles, 52, of Largo. "It wasn't like he didn't go to the doctor. It's not like he didn't seek care. He did. Repeatedly."

Dangel said the facility has had no preventable deaths linked to delays in getting consults with specialists.

"Early diagnosis of cancer and other medical conditions does not always occur," said Dangel. "As hard as trained medical professionals work to ensure the very best outcomes for patients, deaths will occur. This is true inside and outside the VA."

Last month, Gov. Rick Scott ordered the Florida Agency for Health Care Administration to inspect VA hospitals in the state because of concerns about inadequate care. The state inspectors were turned away, the VA says, because they have no jurisdiction in a federal hospital.

ShutDownTheVA@gmail.com

Lalley, who was a retired grocery sales broker, loved the Young VA and its health care professionals.

"That was the only hospital where he wanted to go," Voyles said. "My dad loved going there so he could talk to other veterans about being in the service. He just loved it. And he thought he was getting wonderful care."

A review of Lalley's medical records show he suffered from persistent symptoms that his primary care doctor said were caused by urinary tract infections, or UTIs.

Lalley's symptoms go back more than a decade. On Nov. 9, 2004, Lalley "woke up urinating bright red blood," according to his medical file. He visited the VA hospital, and his doctor noted Lalley had a "history of UTIs several years ago."

But by his next visit, Lalley's symptoms had abated. A note from a Dec. 16, 2004, exam noted his UTI had "resolved."

ShutDownTheVA@gmail.com

Story #15

2008

Veteran Medical Malpractice: Misdiagnosed Cancer[26]

May 15, 2008, 4:00AM. By Jane Mundy

Fayetteville, NC

When William complained about stomach pains Alice B. took her husband to the VA hospital on several occasions, but he was sent home with heartburn medicine. Finally she took him to a civilian hospital: the diagnosis was pancreatic cancer and the diagnosis for the VA hospital was *Veteran Medical Malpractice*: the cancer clinic said it was too late for treatment.

"William started getting stomach pains in August of 2007 and I took him to the VA hospital several times for the same complaint," says Alice. "That went on for about four months but they told William that he "just had gastritis".

---

[26] https://www.lawyersandsettlements.com/legal-news/veteran_medical_malpractice/veteran-medical-malpractice-misdiagnosis-10617.html

ShutDownTheVA@gmail.com

When he got really bad, about two months before he died, the doctors at the VA hospital finally did a CT scan and found a 'pseudo cyst'. I had not idea what that meant so I looked it up on the internet's medical pages and read that it was a fake cyst; something was there but they weren't sure. The doctors said they would check it again in a few months.

But William was hurting really bad so I took him to my family doctor. He said another CT Scan was needed, but this time at a private facility so we got that done. Before I got home that very day, they had called and said William had pancreatic cancer. They told me to get all the records I could because there had to be a needle biopsy done so I went back to the VA and in the middle of all this, the VA wanted him to have a colonoscopy done right away but they didn't have doctors on staff to do it so they told me to take him to another specialist. But when the specialist saw the results of the CT Scan from the private clinic, he said there were things going on that were more important and it wasn't necessary.

I went back to the VA and the doctor said the results of this CT Scan didn't mean anything! My sister is a nurse and she kept all the medical records and documents. I had the paperwork from the gastrointestinal doctor that said his cancer count was over 8,000. (Apparently a normal range is supposed to be no more than 200 —which means you don't have any cancer.)

Then the VA decided to send him to Chapel Hill, NC to do a needle biopsy. It is a civilian hospital and William was transported back to the VA by ambulance. This was in November. Because the VA brought him back, it was clear that they were supposed to take care of the bill.

Yesterday in the mail I got a letter from the hospital in Chapel Hill and they took part of my tax refund to pay for the biopsy. I just called the VA hospital and evidently they didn't take care of the paperwork and only filed his Medicare. The VA is supposed to pay for all of it.

When My husband was 72—he was healthy and athletic and the doctor said he could have lived another 10 years, if not for this cancer.

I've got to the point where I can't talk about it without crying. When we got the results of the biopsy, he went to the cancer clinic right away—he had hope. But they said it was too late, there was nothing they could do to help. William also lost 75 lbs in three months. You wouldn't believe how he looked—it was so terrible.

Before we knew it, the end was there. We only knew for a few weeks exactly what it was, after I took him to my family doctor. I know there is no cure for pancreatic cancer but he wasn't treated right from the beginning with this awful disease. I had to beg the VA to get a needle biopsy, because no cancer doctor would do any kind of treatments until we had it. Finally, about six weeks before he died (still thinking it was gastritis) they sent him to Chapel Hill for the biospy. I am so mad at how he died, still thinking it was not cancer till the very end. The VA should have to pay in some form or another."

Read More at LawyersandSettlements.com

ShutDownTheVA@gmail.com

Story #16

2015

Vet sues VA for \$50M, says it misdiagnosed cancer[27]

Anya Rogers, The Republic | azcentral.com

Published 7:59 a.m. MT Nov. 9, 2015 | Updated 8:01 a.m. MT Nov. 9, 2015

A Phoenix veteran is suing the VA Medical Center for \$50 million in damages, saying he received a late diagnosis of terminal prostate cancer.

His suit comes after years of complaints about the Phoenix VA facility and its urology care. According to a civil complaint filed in U.S. District Court, Steven Cooper, 44,

---

[27]

https://www.azcentral.com/story/news/local/phoenix/2015/11/09/phoenix-vet-sues-va-50-million-says-misdiagnosed-deadly-cancer/74750646/

served in the Army for 18 years before he was honorably discharged in 2007. The complaint states that between July and December 2011, Cooper attempted to schedule an appointment with the Carl T. Hayden VA Medical Center.

He could only schedule the appointment for months later, but his appointment was canceled many times by the VA, forcing him to reschedule, according to the complaint.

When Cooper came to his appointment on Dec. 17, 2011, he was seen by a nurse practitioner, not a physician. The nurse practitioner failed to properly examine, evaluate, diagnose and treat Cooper when she noticed he had an asymmetrical prostate, but did not advise him to seek further care, according to the complaint.

The complaint says Cooper continued to seek medical care throughout 2012 for the symptoms he had made the original appointment for.

According to the complaint, it was not until December 2012 that a VA Medical Center doctor ordered a prostate-specific antigen test for Cooper. When the results were abnormal, a biopsy was performed on Cooper's prostate on Dec. 14, 2012. The complaint says Cooper met with a urology doctor on Dec. 21, 2012 and was informed that he had stage four prostate cancer and was advised to seek hospice care.

Cooper sought a second opinion, according to the complaint, and he received a radical prostatectomy three weeks later. The complaint says he suffered complications and is now terminally ill.

ShutDownTheVA@gmail.com

Cooper filed his lawsuit against the VA on Oct. 26, seeking $50 million for "personal injuries due to medical negligence."

Cooper declined to speak with a reporter, directing questions to his attorney, Greg Patton.

"Steve was a successful independent business owner ... and his expected lifetime earnings would be $25 million," Patton said. "The other $25 million is the value of Steve's life."

Cooper had no insurance, according to Patton, and his only option for health care was the VA medical system. Patton said Cooper was told by the nurse practitioner that he had no reason to be concerned about his abnormal exam and that further treatment was not necessary.

According to Patton, the nurse practitioner was wrong, and had Cooper received the proper medical care during his visit in 2011, his prostate cancer would not have advanced as far as it did.

Since scandal erupted in April 2014, when VA employees complained about a months-long waiting list for ailing veterans, the Carl T. Hayden VA Medical Center has been under a microscope.

The problems with wait times at the center were due to a lack of space and lack of staffing, according to Jean Schaefer, a public affairs officer.

"We have taken steps to address both of those," Schaefer said in a phone interview Monday.

According to a report released by the VA Office of the Inspector General on Oct. 15, 45 percent of patients at the Phoenix center with bladder, prostate or urinary-tract issues received delayed care, or no care at all, during the past two years.

The report described 10 cases where patients' treatment or diagnosis was so delayed that it "may have affected their clinical outcomes" and that, "such delays placed patients at unnecessary risk."
In half of those 10 cases, the patients died.

Schaefer said in an e-mail that since 2014, the VA has increased the "number of employees in urology to 6.5 full-time-equivalent employees and are actively recruiting two more employees."

Schaefer and the VA declined to comment specifically on Cooper's case.

Read or Share this story: http://azc.cc/1iNWmq3
2 of 2 11/21/2019, 9:40 AM

ShutDownTheVA@gmail.com

Guinea Pigs

ShutDownTheVA@gmail.com

Story #17

2019

This next story is compiled from a series of sources, inspired by a *Guardian* newspaper story reported by Peter Cary, one of the world's most respected journalist.

Trump's praise put drug for vets on fast track, but experts aren't sure it works 28

Published — June 18, 2019

Stakes are high for pharmaceutical giant Johnson & Johnson; did company's relationship with president's buddies, VA give drug a boost?

This story from PublicInegrity.com was published in partnership with The Guardian. Peter Cary Reporter

Introduction

---

[28] https://publicintegrity.org/federal-politics/trumps-raves-put-drug-for-vets-on-fast-track-but-experts-arent-sure-it-works/

On March 5, 2019, President Trump signed an executive order to create a "national roadmap to empower veterans and end suicide." That same day, the U.S. Food and Drug Administration approved a new drug called Spravato for treatment of depression and suicidal intent. And over the next 24 to 48 hours, staffers at the Department of Veterans Affairs (VA) were flooded with requests and orders regarding the previously unknown drug because, they were told by one of their bosses, the President himself thought Spravato would be terrific for the VA. Another official was heard to say that President Trump wanted the VA to buy "truckloads" of the drug.

The suggestion of White House interest stoked Washington's special brand of bureaucratic chaos. By week's end, more than 20 people at the Veterans Health Administration (VHA), which runs the VA's medical centers, had kicked into high gear to get Spravato to patients. Within two weeks, likely a record for the usually lumbering approval process, the VHA was announcing that the drug would be made available to vets. By the end of March, scores of physicians would be involved.

Update
The drug was getting great press too; *The Washington Post* and Bloomberg, among others, aired claims that Spravato, whose formal name is esketamine, was a new, fast-acting answer for treatment- resistant depression — a wonder drug. Five FDA officials who were involved in its approval, writing in the prestigious New England Journal of Medicine, called it "a novel treatment for a severe and life-threatening

condition," touting its "rapid onset of effect [as] a key benefit."

But not everyone was convinced — far from it. The drug's heightened profile has unleashed a storm of questions from academics, psychiatrists, and health researchers who have concerns about Spravato: how it was approved, how well it works, whether it is safe, how much it costs, and whether it's right for veterans. The discussion has surfaced some unsettling concerns:

The FDA abandoned a longstanding procedure of requiring two successful short-term trials before approving anti-depression drugs. Instead, when this drug showed itself to be no better than placebo in two of three short-term trials, the FDA accepted the one successful trial, adding on another and different type of trial that some say was deeply flawed.

Even though the drug is being hurried into use by the VA, some psychiatrists and researchers say the evidence from trials does not demonstrate that the drug is effective on people over 65 — or possibly even on males. The VA's patient population is 90 percent male and 52 percent over 65. During several years of trials, six people who had been treated with the drug died, as opposed to none on placebos. Three of the deaths were suicides. The FDA said it was difficult to conclude that the deaths were caused by the drug. Still, noted one psychiatrist, "It's not heading in the direction supporting protection from suicides."

Data from the drug's trials shows it to be only slightly better than placebos in its performance. "The benefit isn't much,"

ShutDownTheVA@gmail.com

said Julie Zito, professor emerita of pharmacy and psychiatry at the University of Maryland, who cast one of the two no votes on the FDA advisory committee that approved the drug.

The dangers of treatment— mainly dissociation, hallucinations, sleepiness, and blood-pressure hikes — are so significant that patients must stay in the doctor's office for two hours after receiving their Spravato infusion. The office must be equipped with equipment to deal with hallucinatory, cardiac, and respiratory problems. "A wonder drug? I think it's a wonder that anybody thinks it's a wonder drug," said Diana Zuckerman, president of the National Center for Health Research, a nonpartisan institute that studies science and health in Washington, DC.

How the president learned of the drug and how exactly his enthusiasm was communicated to the VA remains a mystery. The White House declined to answer questions on that subject, as did the VA. Johnson & Johnson, and its subsidiary Janssen Pharmaceuticals which makes the drug, had been partnering with the VA on anti-suicide programs as Spravato was being developed. J&J was also working with a trio of Trump associates from his Mar-a-Lago club who have influenced VA policies. The three associates did not return phone calls and messages from the Center. But Spravato's momentum continues. Last week Bloomberg reported that Trump, in a meeting with VA Secretary Robert Wilkie, offered to help the VA negotiate purchases of the drug from Janssen. Trump trumpeted the drug's efficacy, saying, "You have people calling for help and if those people

ShutDownTheVA@gmail.com

had that, I'm hearing like instantaneously they're in better shape."

VA Secretary Robert Wilkie, left, is seen with President Trump on Nov. 11, 2018 at the White House as the president signs a Veterans Day message. Bloomberg reported that, in a meeting with Wilkie last week, Trump offered to help the VA negotiate purchases of the drug Spravato from maker Janssen Pharmaceuticals.

The VA declined to answer specific questions or grant interviews about the drug, its appropriateness for VA patients, and its hurried rush through the approval process. It provided a brief statement saying it "has approved the use of intranasal esketamine for adults with treatment-resistant depression (when used in conjunction with an oral antidepressant)." The statement went on to say that the "VA has not yet administered esketamine to any patients and is in the process of designing a clinical implementation plan optimized for safety and efficacy." The FDA declined to answer questions about the drug, its trials, or the approval process, referring a reporter to that article written by its officials for the New England Journal of Medicine.

The stakes are considerable. For Johnson & Johnson, facing an opioid-distribution trial in Oklahoma that may cost millions, Spravato could be a blockbuster: Analysts estimate it could earn $600 million by 2022. This week a VA committee will meet to decide whether to add the drug to its formulary — the list of drugs that must be available to VA pharmacies. If the drug is placed on the formulary, it could be a real boon for J&J's marketing of Spravato. If the drug

ShutDownTheVA@gmail.com

is not put on the formulary, doctors can still prescribe it "off-formulary" but the drug will lack the VA's imprimatur. For veterans whose ranks are plagued by depression and suicides, much is at stake too. A drug that offers fast and lasting answer for treatment-resistant depression would be a godsend. But is this drug the answer?

A twisted history

Spravato is a derivative of ketamine, which was approved by the FDA in 1970 and licensed to Par Pharmaceuticals. Due to its hallucinogenic properties, it was used as an anesthetic for large animals, but it was also abused as a club drug known as "Special K." In the 1990s a team of researchers at Yale tested it on seven patients with depression, and found that it worked, and fast — within a few hours. (Some scientists think Ketamine releases glutamate, which promotes the growth of neural connections in the brain that aid reasoning and pleasurable feelings.) Frustrated doctors turned to ketamine injections as an off-label drug of last resort for treatment-resistant depression, and ketamine clinics sprung up nationwide. Veterans Health Administration doctors give it to desperate patients, though not in large numbers.

The anti-depressant drug Spravato is delivered via a nasal inhaler. The drug can produce serious side effects, such as disconnection from surroundings, sedation, dizziness, and high blood pressure, and patients must stay in their doctor's - office for two hours after treatment. (Janssen Pharmaceutical Companies of Johnson & Johnson)

ShutDownTheVA@gmail.com

Ketamine's dangers, too, have been well known — dissociation (an out-of-body feeling), sedation, suicidal thoughts, and hiked blood pressure are not unusual. Indeed, in April, 2017 a group of eight psychiatrists from an American Psychiatric Council task force wrote a consensus statement in JAMA Psychiatry saying there was an "urgent need for guidance" on ketamine use, citing "unanswered questions and concerns."

Ketamine is off patent, meaning that it is readily available. Drug companies typically do not want to invest research dollars to find a new use for a drug they cannot patent. But the folks at Janssen Pharmaceuticals had an idea. Ketamine, like many drugs, consists of compounds of two attached molecules that are mirror images. It is possible to make a new drug of just one of the two molecules that has similar but not identical effects of the original. In this case, Janssen created a drug of only left-side ketamine molecules and called it esketamine. They also developed it as a nasal spray to avoid injection.

Janssen took esketamine into Phase I clinical trials, with small patient numbers taking small doses to test its safety. In November 2013 the FDA granted it Breakthrough Therapy Designation — meaning that early trials indicate the drug may offer substantial treatment advantages, and so it gets priority FDA review. Janssen then moved into Phase 2 trials, which involve more patients and require longer monitoring. During these tests, in a trial called SYNAPSE 2003, a 41-year-old male patient committed suicide by hanging. He had taken esketamine 20 days earlier.

ShutDownTheVA@gmail.com

In August 2016, based on the results of the phase 2 trials, the FDA granted esketamine another Breakthrough Therapy Designation, and Janssen moved into Phase 3 trials designed to test esketamine's effects against those of a placebo. There were more patients — more than 1,700 in all worldwide, the majority being Caucasian women. Janssen also launched a so-called "withdrawal" trial, in which patients on esketamine were taken off to see how long it would take them to return to their previous condition.

Some longer-term trials were started too. Two of the patients in those trials committed suicide. One man, 38, three days off of esketamine, shot himself. Another, a 55 year old woman, 13 days off esketamine, killed herself with a multi-drug overdose. There were other deaths as well: a 41-year-old man, 26 hours off esketamine in a short-term trial, died in a motorcycle accident. Two esketamine takers died in the longer-term trials: one, 60, of cardiac and respiratory failure and the other, 74, of myocardial infarction. They had been off esketamine for 5 and 6 days respectively. Janssen said in a statement that "six deaths occurred, although none were considered by investigators to be related to Spravato." The FDA would later say that given the small number of deaths and the severity of subjects' depression, "it is difficult to consider these deaths as drug-related." However, an equal number of patients received placebos in these trials. None of them died.

"Disturbingly, the FDA appears to inappropriately discount the possibility that these suicides were linked to esketamine exposure," wrote the watchdog group Public Citizen. It had sent the FDA a 14-page letter on February 27, 2019 urging that the drug not be approved without more research, citing unproven efficacy and proven dangers.

"Disturbingly, the FDA appears to inappropriately discount the possibility that these suicides were linked to esketamine exposure."

Letter from watchdog group public citizen

As the Phase 3 trials moved forward, Johnson & Johnson began a relationship with the Department of Veterans Affairs and that trio of civilian advisers who were associated with President Trump through social club Mar-a-Lago. The three, Marvel Entertainment Chairman Ike Perlmutter, Palm Beach physician Bruce Moskowitz, and attorney Marc Sherman, were labeled the "Mar-a-Lago Council" in a 2018 lawsuit by a veterans group against the VA, alleging that the group operated as an illegal advisory committee and had an outsized influence over President Trump's decisions regarding the VA. Much of the lawsuit was based on an article by ProPublica. (The VA has moved to dismiss the suit, saying the trio were just individuals giving advice.)

The suit claims the trio convened a series of conference calls with J&J executives to discuss and promote a public awareness campaign about veteran suicides; as part of that effort, then-VA secretary David Shulkin was joined by J&J officials and characters from Perlmutter's company, Marvel, to ring the closing bell on Veterans Day, 2017, at the New York Stock Exchange.

Johnson & Johnson joined then-VA Secretary David Shulkin and Disney to ring the closing bell of the New York Stock

ShutDownTheVA@gmail.com

Exchange on Veterans Day, Nov. 7, 2017. Some ask if it was appropriate for J&J to be partnering with the VA as it developed a drug that it hoped to sell to the agency. (New York Stock Exchange)

In responding to ProPublica's queries, the trio cited Perlmutter's "personal relationship with the President" and said they "offered our counsel, and the advice of these healthcare experts, to assist the President, Secretary and VA leadership in their making the essential decisions." They said this was done voluntarily, "seeking nothing at all in return."

As trials for the drug went forward in late 2017, J&J also joined the VA's suicide prevention program, #BeThere. Johnson & Johnson's website says that in 2018 and beyond the company will work with the VA to "undertake new clinical trial processes in hopes of providing access to the latest and most innovative treatments to help veterans in need."

Records from the Center for Responsive Politics show that J&J was among the firms lobbying most heavily at the VA in 2018; records show J&J lobbying the VA on matters including "partnership with the VA on suicide prevention." CRP records show that J&J spent a total of $6.6 million that year lobbying the federal government and hired a dozen lobbying firms to help. Employees of the company gave $14,165 to Trump's 2016 campaign.

ShutDownTheVA@gmail.com

Relationships

Courtney Billington, a former Army captain and President, Neurosciences, of Janssen Pharmaceuticals, noted on the J&J website that Johnson & Johnson had a 115-year history of working with the military and "is uniquely positioned to reach, engage and empower the public to support the heroes in our communities." In 2013 J&J CEO Alex Gorsky rang the opening bell at the stock exchange on Veterans Day with members of the U.S. Military Academy.

Asked if Janssen or J&J had a conflict of interest in partnering with the VA on anti-suicide programs while developing an anti-suicide drug it planned to sell to the VA, Janssen said in a statement that throughout the partnership, "we've had a memorandum of understanding in place that we've followed, and have strictly complied with the laws in place that govern partnerships across industry and government related to ethics and conflicts of interest." It also said its work with the VA "does not involve any exchange of funds."

Michael Carome, director of Public Citizen's Health Research Group, took a different view of the partnership and the intended sale of the drug: "The circumstances you describe are disturbing and the conduct of the VA is unseemly," he said.

When the Phase 3 trials were finished, the FDA called a joint meeting of its Psychopharmacologic Drugs Advisory Committee and Drug Safety and Risk Management Advisory committees on February 12, 2019, with 17 voting members present or on the phone. Janssen and FDA officials

ShutDownTheVA@gmail.com

each presented hundreds of pages of material on the esketamine trials.

The vote of an advisory committee, with members who are clinicians or research experts in the field, is normally the last step before the FDA approves or disapproves a drug. The panels have long been controversial; a 2006 study by the National Research Center for Women & Families (now the National Center for Health Research) found that many of the committees approved almost every product they reviewed, that they bowed to pressure to conform, and they typically voted the way they sensed the FDA wanted them to vote.

In this case, the joint committee voted 14-2 with one abstention to approve the drug for release. Committee member Walter Dunn, mood disorder director at the West Los Angeles Veterans Administration Medical Center, a yes vote, told the panels "there is compelling evidence that esketamine is an effective treatment for this highly treatment-resistant population."

But the vote was met with skepticism from some of the committee members and from more than a few outside psychiatrists and researchers. They zeroed in on the data from the trials. The trials themselves barely proved efficacy, they said, or even rapid action. The trials also did not show that the drug worked on patients over 65, nor, some argued, even on males. And the suicides concerned them.

The FDA's acceptance of just one short-term trial, and replacement of the second short-term trial with another kind of trial, had not previously been done, the agency admitted, but was "not unreasonable." FDA committee member Erick

ShutDownTheVA@gmail.com

Turner of the Oregon Health and Science University, who did not make the meeting, called that FDA position "bullshit." "It's not a reason," said Turner, a former FDA drug reviewer. "It's like a parent saying, 'Because I said so.'" Diana Zuckerman, president of the National Center for Health Research in Washington, DC, said the reason two trials are normally required is to show that results can be replicated. "It's science," she said.

Turner, Zuckerman, and Jess Fiedorowicz, an associate psychiatry professor at the University of Iowa who also works at the VA Medical Center-Iowa City, all had problems with the second trial the FDA accepted, saying, among other things, that it allowed patients to figure out whether they were on esketamine or the placebo. They also pointed out that the one short-term trial with patients over 65, a so-called "geriatric trial," was unsuccessful. This and contentions from some that the trials did not demonstrate the drug's effectiveness on men raised questions about its usefulness to the VA — whose patients are mostly male and over 65. Fiedorowicz said he wasn't sure about the data on males, but it didn't matter. "We have not even shown that the medication works," he said. He chose to abstain from voting because the FDA approved the design of the trials.

Still, with the 14-2-1 advisory committee vote in hand, the FDA approved esketamine, with the trade name Spravato, on March 5. "There has been a long-standing need for additional effective treatments for treatment-resistant depression, a serious and life-threatening condition," said Tiffany Farchione, M.D., acting director of the Division of

ShutDownTheVA@gmail.com

Psychiatry Products in the FDA's Center for Drug Evaluation and Research, in a press release.

On the same day, President Trump, who has claimed to champion veterans issues, signed an executive order on a National Roadmap to Empower Veterans and End Suicide. The seven-page document talked of a plan to "empower veterans and end suicide through coordinated suicide prevention efforts, prioritized research activities, and strengthened collaboration across the public and private sectors."

President Donald J. Trump signs an executive order for a "National Roadmap to Empower Veterans and End a National Tragedy of Suicide – the PREVENTS Initiative" Tuesday, March 5, 2019, in the Roosevelt Room of the White House. That same day, the Food and Drug Administration approved the drug Spravato.

Within 24 to 48 hours, according to VA sources, agency staffers were scrambling after hearing that the president was urging them to buy Spravato in "truckloads." Briefings were hastily prepared, and early morning meetings called. Staffers scoured their regions to find out what clinics, if any, were outfitted to handle esketamine treatment, and what would have to be done to add more clinics to the list. A contract with Janssen Pharmaceuticals was signed in 48 hours so that pricing could be nailed down. Normally such a contract takes a month or more. Patient consent paperwork was prepared. VA officials created Powerpoints, and a lengthy and detailed paper on the drug, its applications and uses and dangers was rushed into print. Efforts were initiated to equip new clinics to handle esketamine treatments. The press office began work on a statement.

On March 19 — two weeks after the FDA approved the drug — the VA announced that Spravato would be available for its patients. Its press release quoted Secretary Wilkie: "We're pleased to be able to expand options for veterans with depression who have not responded to other treatments." Staffers were told the goal was to treat the first VA patient with Spravato within 90 days.

But the debate over Spravato has not abated. On May 17, three psychiatrists, Michael D. Alpert and J. Wesley Boyd at Harvard Medical School, and Marco A. Ramos at Yale, published a piece at Vice.com headlined, "The New Ketamine-Based Antidepressant Is a Rip-Off." The authors noted the cost of the drug, "nearly $900 per dose, or roughly $7000 for the first months of treatment," and that the drug proved to be no better than placebo in two of its three short-term trials.

But "the biggest problem at hand is not the drug itself," they added. "It's the fact that instead of representing a revolution in mental health treatment, as it has been touted to do, esketamine is not a breakthrough at all."

By week's end, it will be clear whether the VA's formulary committee agrees.

Ashley Lin Wong contributed to this story.

ShutDownTheVA@gmail.com

Contributions & Sources

The Guardian is an excellent newspaper from the United Kingdom. It also keeps offices in the United States, often reporting on events here.

In this oversaturated media world we live in today, The Guardian offers unbiased reporting funded by the readers. That's right, you can support their journalism with your contributions. Please visit their website today.

ShutDownTheVA@gmail.com

Veteran Suicides

ShutDownTheVA@gmail.com

Story #18

2019

Suicides on VA properties sound the alarm on veteran care[29]

By Dean Reynolds CBS News May 8, 2019, 6:41 PM

St. Paul, Minn. — On average, about 20 veterans a day die by suicide. Since 2017, 25 veterans have taken their lives on the grounds of Veterans Affairs hospitals, including seven this year and at least four last month.

In February of last year, Justin Miller died by suicide in the parking lot of a Veterans Administration hospital in Minneapolis. The Marine veteran was 33. Justin, a trumpet player, made the band, but the Marines saw he could make another contribution as a marksman in Iraq manning a checkpoint with bomb-sniffing dogs.

---

[29] https://www.cbsnews.com/news/united-states-military-veteran-suicides-on-veterans-affairs-properties-sound-the-alarm-on-veteran-care/

ShutDownTheVA@gmail.com

"If the dog sat down, pull the trigger. Those were his orders. And he said he did that for weeks, day in, day out," said Gregory Miller, Justin's father.

Veterans and suicide risk: The warning signs — and how to get help

When he left the Marines in 2007, his family said he changed. While he still volunteered to play his trumpet at various occasions, he was increasingly depressed and even suicidal. Eventually he sought help at a Veterans Affairs hospital.

"We said we loved each other. I kissed him, and that was the last time I saw my son," Miller said.

After three days at the VA, he died.

"He went out to his car. He looked at his phone. He saw the text from my dad, saying 'I love you. Come home.' And at some point he took his own life," said Alissa Harrington, Justin's sister.

Experts in this field say veterans who kill themselves on VA grounds are making a statement about their treatment. A federal investigation of Miller's death said the Minneapolis VA made multiple mistakes, from not scheduling a follow-up to overlooking his access to firearms.

"They have people, but they're not trained the way they're supposed to be," Miller said.

ShutDownTheVA@gmail.com

Some 6,000 veterans kill themselves every year. VA Secretary Robert Wilkie, whose department serves 9.5 million people, said in the last year, they have had 240 interventions where they stopped veterans from taking their lives. Since October, the VA has screened 900,000 veterans for mental health issues.

"Of that 900,000 we culled it down to 3,000. Three thousands veterans our medical professionals say might be at risk and we are monitoring them as closely as we can," Wilkie said. "That means calls, that means visits — bringing them into our centers."

In Miller's case, antidepressants came in the mail from the VA two days after he died. "The worst part of his funeral was that they didn't have a live trumpet player. There was no one there to play for him," Harrington said.

The silent trumpet at his grave was a gift from his dad.

© 2019 CBS Interactive Inc. All Rights Reserved.

Story #19

2008

Veterans are committing suicide in VA parking lots[30]

The Washington Post investigation focused on a few specific cases, including the February 2018 suicide of 33-year-old Marine Corps veteran Justin Miller in the Minneapolis VA hospital's parking lot. (Jim Mone/AP)

By: Joshua Axelrod   February 7
A new report illustrates a troubling trend of veterans committing suicide on VA hospital campuses after receiving inadequate care from individual facilities.

Nineteen suicides have occurred on VA campuses from October 2017 to November 2018 — seven of them in parking lots, according to data the Washington Post obtained from the Department of Veterans Affairs. Some are worried

---

[30]

https://rebootcamp.militarytimes.com/news/transition/2019/02/08/veterans-are-committing-suicide-in-va-parking-lots-report/

that this is a gruesome form of protest by veterans to highlight how little help they were given in their time of need by the VA system.

On Thursday, the Post published an investigation into this phenomenon featuring both big-picture concerns about mental-health services offered by the Department of Veterans Affairs and stories about veterans who took their lives after attempting to get treatment from their local VA hospitals.

The Post investigation focused on a few specific cases, including the February 2018 suicide of 33-year-old Marine Corps veteran Justin Miller in the Minneapolis VA hospital's parking lot, as well as 32-year-old former Army Sgt. John Toombs, who hung himself on the grounds of a VA medical center in Murfreesboro, Tennessee, just before Thanksgiving 2016.

Both men entered the separate VA facilities seeking assistance for post-traumatic stress disorder stemming from their time in the military, among other issues. Miller killed himself after four days in the Minneapolis VA's mental-health unit, and Toombs did the same after being kicked out of his treatment program for not following its instructions, including being 20 minutes late to pick up his medications. Most recently, 55-year-old Marine Col. Jim Turner shot himself in December 2018 outside the Bay Pines Department of Veterans Affairs while dressed in his service uniform. He left a disturbing note that investigators found close to his body: "I bet if you look at the 22 suicides a day you will see VA screwed up in 90 percent."

There were more than 6,000 reported veteran suicides every year from 2008-16, according to the 2005-16 VA National Suicide Data Report. The same report indicated that as of 2016, the suicide rate for veterans was 1.5 times higher than for non-veteran adults.

In January 2018, President Donald Trump signed an executive order to give all veterans access to mental-health services for the entire first year of their new civilian lives. The VA told the Washington Post that it prevented 233 suicide attempts in that October 2017-November 2018 window, which mainly involved VA staff stopping veterans from hurting themselves on their campuses.

The quality of care at individual VA facilities fluctuates wildly, as demonstrated by the Department of Veteran Affairs' 2016 Quality of Care report that ranks each hospital in various categories. The one that Toombs entered in Murfreesboro happened to be one of the lowest-ranked in the entire VA system for its mental-health care.

Miller's suicide invoked an official inquiry into the failings of the Minneapolis VA system that may have led to his death. The VA Office of the Inspector General determined that the facility staff who evaluated Miller did not schedule any follow-up appointments, communicate with his family about his treatment plan and, most crucially, properly assess his access to firearms.

ShutDownTheVA@gmail.com

"The VA didn't cause his suicide," Alissa Harrington, Miller's sister, told the Washington Post. "But they could have done more to prevent that, and that's just so maddening."

ShutDownTheVA@gmail.com

Story #20

2019

My thanks for permission to reprint this story from all the sources listed at the end of the story.

Three Veterans in Five Days Die by Suicide at VA Facilities[31]

13 Apr 2019
Stars and Stripes | By Nikki Wentling
WASHINGTON -- Three suicides occurred during a five-day period on Department of Veterans Affairs properties, prompting reaction this week from Capitol Hill.

Two veterans died by suicide in Georgia, one April 5 at a parking garage at the Carl Vinson VA Medical Center in Dublin and the other April 6 outside the main entrance to the Atlanta VA Medical Center in Decatur, the Atlanta Journal-Constitution reported.

---

[31] https://www.military.com/daily-news/2019/04/13/three-veterans-five-days-die-suicide-va-facilities.html

On Tuesday, a veteran shot himself in the waiting room at a VA clinic in Austin, Texas, according to KWCX-TV.

"Those deaths did not go by me without noticing them, nor has it gone by me that we have a job to do," Sen. Johnny Isakson, R-Ga., said Wednesday during a Senate Veterans' Affairs Committee hearing.

Though it wasn't the intended subject of the hearing, multiple senators asked VA officials on Wednesday about the recent suicides.

Richard Stone, executive in charge of the Veterans Health Administration, said there have been more than 260 suicide attempts on VA property, 240 of which were interrupted and prevented. He didn't specify a time period for the attempts.

According to a Washington Post report, 19 suicides occurred on VA property between October 2017 and November 2018. "Every one of these is a gut-wrenching experience for our 24,000 mental health providers and all of us that work for VA," Stone said.

In response to reports of the three suicides, Rep. Mark Takano, D-Calif., chairman of the House Committee on Veterans' Affairs, said he would schedule a hearing on the issue later this month.

"Every new instance of veteran suicide showcases a barrier to access, but with three incidents on VA property in just five days, and six this year alone, it's critical we do more to stop this epidemic," Takano said in a statement. "I have called for

ShutDownTheVA@gmail.com

a full committee hearing... to hear from VA about the recent tragedies and spark a larger discussion about what actions we can take together as a nation."

According to the latest VA data, 20 veterans die by suicide every day. Of those deaths, 14 are not receiving VA health care.

Suicide among veterans continues to be higher than the rest of the population, and younger veterans are particularly at risk. VA data released in September showed the rate of suicide among veterans ages 18 to 34 had significantly increased.

The VA hasn't identified the veterans who died by suicide in Georgia, nor described the circumstances of the deaths. In Austin, a still-unidentified veteran shot himself in front of hundreds of people in the waiting room, KWTX reported. Weapons are prohibited in VA clinics, but the Austin facility didn't have metal detectors.

Stone told senators Wednesday that veteran suicide was a societal problem that needed a nationwide approach. He noted an executive order that President Donald Trump signed in March creating a Cabinet-level task force that he promised would "mobilize every level of American society" to address veteran suicide. VA Secretary Robert Wilkie was selected to lead it.

"I wish it was as simple as me saying I could do more patrols in a parking lot that would stop this epidemic," Stone said.

ShutDownTheVA@gmail.com

"Where we as a community and society have failed that veteran is a very complex answer."

This article is written by Nikki Wentling from Stars and Stripes and was legally licensed via the Tribune Content Agency through the NewsCred publisher network.

Related Topics
Military Headlines
Department of Veterans Affairs - VA
Suicide Prevention

© Copyright 2019 Stars and Stripes. All rights reserved.

ShutDownTheVA@gmail.com

Story #21

2019

Chairman Takano Reaction to New VA Data on Veteran Suicide [32]

September 20, 2019

WASHINGTON, D.C. – Today, House Committee on Veterans' Affairs Chairman Mark Takano (CA-41) released the following statement after the Department of Veterans Affairs released their new data detailing suicide rates among veterans in 2017.

"As Chairman of the House Committee on Veterans' Affairs, I've made addressing veteran suicide my top priority-- but these numbers make it clear we're not doing enough. This new data reaffirms the urgent need for Americans to immediately act to address veteran suicide, and it serves as a sobering reminder that we cannot take our minds off this crisis for one second.

---

[32] https://veterans.house.gov/news/press-releases/chairman-takano-reaction-to-new-va-data-on-veteran-suicide-

ShutDownTheVA@gmail.com

"The suicide rate among veterans is 1.5 times higher than the rate for non-veteran adults and sadly, the rate of suicide among women veterans specifically, is more than 2.2 times higher. We must continue to push through and find new, creative solutions to reduce veteran suicide.

"Particularly heartbreaking is the rate at which veterans have died by suicide on VA property. That's why I called for a nation-wide stand-down to ensure all VA staff have the training they need to care for veterans in crisis to assess whether all facilities are equipped with key safety features, and to discern any gaps in policies or procedures that we can fix. We should not look solely to Congress, the VA or our Veteran Service Organizations for all the answers. But I know that together, we can find a way to truly be there for our veterans in crisis."

If you or a veteran you know are struggling, contact the Veteran Crisis Line 24/7 at 1-800-273-8255 and select option 1, or text 838255.

Press Contact

Jenni Geurink (202-225-9756)

Miguel R. Salazar

Story #22

2019

Hours After 7th Vet Suicide at VA, Officials Repeat Plea for Public to Help [33]

This article reprinted with permission of military.com. Please visit their website for more stories www.military.com

30 Apr 2019
Military.com | By Patricia Kime
-- Patricia Kime can be reached at
Patricia.Kime@Military.com.
Follow her on Twitter @patriciakime

On a day when a veteran died by suicide outside a Department of Veterans Affairs Medical Center in Cleveland, lawmakers grilled VA leaders on what they are

---

[33] https://www.military.com/daily-news/2019/04/30/hours-after-7th-vet-suicide-va-officials-repeat-plea-public-help.html

ShutDownTheVA@gmail.com

doing to prevent such deaths, while department officials called for a national approach to reverse the tragic trend.

An unidentified veteran died early Monday morning outside the emergency room of the Louis Stokes VA Medical Center in Ohio, the 7th suicide this year on a VA property and the fourth this month.

Lawmakers pointed to the tragedy while holding a bipartisan press conference on veteran suicides and a rare evening hearing to question VA leaders about their efforts to address the issue.

"One today. Twenty veteran service members, Reserve and National Guard succumb to their invisible wounds every day. ... This is an unconscionable urgent crisis requiring immediate action," said Speaker of the House Nancy Pelosi, D-California.

With the budget at the VA for mental health services topping $8.6 billion, House Veterans Affairs Committee members sought to determine how the funds are being used and why the estimated number of suicides a day -- 20 -- has not declined after years of investment.

"Twenty deaths a day totaling more than 7,300 deaths per year is unacceptable. That's 1,800 more deaths per year than the 5,429 service members who have been killed in action since 2001," said committee chairman Rep. Mark Takano, D-California. "Both numbers are ... further evidence of a frustrating and persistent problem we have failed to address."

ShutDownTheVA@gmail.com

"Our goal should be more than just preventing suicide, it should be helping our veterans to live a life of meaning and joy," said Rep. Phil Roe of Tennessee, the senior Republican on the committee.

According to VA data, the suicide rate for veterans is 1.5 times that of civilian Americans. The number of veterans who died by suicide in 2016 declined slightly from the previous year, from 6,281 in 2015 to 6,079 in 2016. But since the number of veterans in the U.S. also declined, the overall rate has remained stubbornly steady.

Some age groups also are more affected than others: While more veterans from the Vietnam and post-Vietnam era die by suicide, veterans ages 18 to 34 have the highest rate of suicide, at 45 per 100,000 people.

VA officials say that, of the estimated 20 veterans who die each day, an average six are enrolled in the VA's health system and have access to the department's range of services and support. But most, however, don't use VA and some are not eligible for care, include roughly three out of every 20 who are members of the National Guard or Reserve and never federally activated.

Dr. Richard Stone, executive in charge of the Veterans Health Administration, told lawmakers that many former service members are deeply damaged, with 77% having been exposed to combat, and the issue cannot be solved solely through mental health treatment.

"Significant amounts of this relates to personal, financial and relationship problems and loneliness and isolation," he said. "The post-9/11 generation of veterans joined the military knowing they were going to combat. That is a unique individual in America."

Stone said the nation needs a "whole of society approach," one that includes not only government agencies, physicians, mental health providers and social services, but family, friends and neighbors to take part.

Nearly three-quarters of those who attempted suicide said they spent less than an hour thinking about their actions. Roughly one quarter spent less than five minutes. With studies showing that interrupting this thought process actually saves lives, the VA has started a campaign it calls "Be There," urging family members, friends and former colleagues to pick up the phone, text or send a social media message to their veteran.

The act of reaching out is a "strong preventive factor for suicide," VA officials said when they introduced the campaign.

"We want to let people know that the things they do every day ... help people feel less alone. That's what this campaign is about -- encouraging people to be there for each other," former director of the VA's Office of Suicide Prevention Caitlin Thompson said.

Friends don't need to bring up the topic if they are uncomfortable with it; they simply can ask how a veteran is doing, buy them a cup of coffee, help them feel more connected, VA officials said.

They also are encouraged to support from the VA Crisis Line, which can offer support and advice for those worried about a friend or family member. And if the veteran is in immediate danger they shouldn't hesitate to call, Stone said. "There are those that would like to indict the VA in this process. This is not as easy as me having just a few more policemen to go through the parking lots. This is about a whole of society approach that reconnects veterans that are intensely lonely and with a feeling of hopelessness that results in these acts," Stone said.

In March, President Donald Trump signed an executive order creating a Cabinet-level task force to examine the federal response to veteran suicides and make recommendations on improving the support system.

VA Secretary Robert Wilkie serves as chairman of the group, which has been tasked to draft a national plan to address the problem.

Meanwhile, lawmakers have introduced a number of bills on veteran suicides, some of which will be considered Tuesday in a meeting of the House Veterans Affairs health subcommittee.

They include a bill by Rep. Anthony Brindisi, D-New York, to improve hiring for VA suicide prevention coordinators, and a bill by Rep. Max Rose, D-New York, which would

ShutDownTheVA@gmail.com

require the VA to notify Congress within seven days of any suicide or attempted suicide at a VA facility.

Other pieces of proposed legislation include:
A bill by Rep. Conor Lamb, D-Pennsylvania, to promote a "whole health" approach to medical treatment at the VA that includes complementary and alternative therapies.

Legislation from Roe and Rep. Mike Levin, D-California -- the Vet Center Eligibility Expansion Act -- which would give members of the National Guard, Reserve and Coast Guard access to care at certain VA facilities known for individualized care.

The Veterans Equal Access Act, introduced by Rep. Earl Blumenauer, D-Oregon, which aims to increase veterans' options for pain management by allowing VA health care providers to refer veterans to state marijuana programs.

A bill from Sen. Jon Tester, D-Montana, ranking member of the Senate Veterans Affairs Committee, and Sen. Jerry Moran, R-Kansas, that would seek to add mental health professionals at the VA by giving the department direct hiring authority and offering scholarships to mental health professionals to work at Vet Centers.

During the hearing, Rep. Kathleen Rice, D-New York, quizzed officials on access to weapons and whether the VA provided any guidance or services to veterans who would like to reduce their access to firearms.

ShutDownTheVA@gmail.com

"We can't adequately address the issue without talking about firearms," Rice said. "Sixty-nine percent of veterans have completed suicide via firearm. Women veterans are also more likely to utilize a firearm. It's been proven that restricting access may reduce suicide risk. Has the VA studied gun violence in the veteran population?"

VA's National Director of Suicide Prevention Keita Franklin said the VA trains its providers on how to talk to veterans about access to lethal means, including weapons and mass quantities to medication. It also maintains a partnership with the National Shooting and Sports Foundation to train gun shop and range instructors on the issue.

Takano promised that Monday's hearing would be the first of several on suicide among service members and veterans, including a future meeting that would bring VA and Defense Department representatives to testify.

He described the issue as deeply personal: When he was a child, an uncle who was a Vietnam veteran died by suicide. "His suicide still haunts me from time to time to this day," Takano said.

The Veterans Crisis Hotline is staffed 24 hours a day, seven days a week, at 800-273-8255, press 1. Services also are available online at www.veteranscrisisline.net or by text, 838255.

© Copyright 2019 Military.com. All rights reserved. This material may not be published, broadcast, rewritten or redistributed.

ShutDownTheVA@gmail.com

Related content:

- VA Won't Ramp Up Security After Rash of Suicides on Premises. Here's Why.
- Wilkie: Entire Government to Focus on Reducing Vet Suicides
- VA Struggles to Curb 'Parking Lot' Suicides at Its Own Facilities
- Three Veterans in Five Days Die by Suicide at VA Facilities
- Senators Want Answers on Unspent VA Suicide Prevention Funds

ShutDownTheVA@gmail.com

Story #23

2019

Veteran's suicide at Florida cemetery raises additional concerns over VA outreach, response[34]

This article reprinted with the kind permission of militarytimes.com. Please visit their website for more stories and to thank them for helping keep veterans informed, www.militarytimes.com

By: Leo Shane III
October 28
Another suicide on a Veterans Affairs campus in Florida earlier this month was the 35th such death at a public department space in less than two years, but officials insist it still does not represent a trend among struggling veterans. The death, which happened at the Bay Pines National Cemetery, occurred the week of Oct. 7, less than 20 days after VA facilities nationwide conducted a "stand down" to

---

[34] https://www.militarytimes.com/news/pentagon-congress/2019/10/28/veterans-suicide-at-florida-cemetery-raises-additional-concerns-over-va-outreach-response/

ShutDownTheVA@gmail.com

discuss new outreach and emergency response protocols with staff. Part of that work was designed to help employees intervene with veterans in public spaces on VA campuses who may be showing signs of suicidal behavior.

The cemetery sits on the sprawling VA campus just northwest of St. Petersburg and is about a 10-minute walk from the Bay Pines VA medical center. The two sites share security and emergency response staff, with personnel conducting rounds throughout the area for signs of problematic activity or veterans in need of assistance.

New veteran suicide numbers raise concerns among experts hoping for positive news

About 17 veterans a day die by suicide, a number that has stayed steady over a decade.

Local officials released few details of the suicide but said they are reviewing site procedures to see if improvements need to be made. But they added that "proper monitoring and response procedures were followed" in this case.

At least six veterans have died by suicide in public areas at Bay Pines in the last six years. The frequency of the incidents — and the face that the deaths are more visible than veterans suicides that occur at home or while in medical care — have drawn increased scrutiny from lawmakers, who are pushing legislation to ensure Congress is informed when any such death occurs.

In the most recent case, that alert did not happen. Officials at the House Veterans' Affairs Committee said they were not

ShutDownTheVA@gmail.com

made aware of the Bay Pines cemetery suicide until being contacted by Military Times.

Members of Congress have also expressed concern that the seemingly increasing number of deaths on VA campuses may point to problems in how employees interact with veterans. But VA officials note that the number of on-campus suicides has decreased in the last few years, even if the number happening in public areas has grown.

VA Press Secretary Christina Mandreucci said since the start of 2018, staff at department campuses have successfully intervened in almost 90 percent of suicide attempts on VA campuses (419 of 466 attempts). Of the 47 deaths, 12 occurred during inpatient care.

"At this time, there is no identified trend demonstrating increasing suicide deaths among veterans in active inpatient care, seeking or recently treated for care, and veterans who die by suicide on VA grounds who are not seeking care," she said.

Earlier this summer, VA Secretary Robert Wilkie testified on Capitol Hill that investigators have found many of the veterans who die by suicide on department campuses choose the site not as a protest against VA, but instead because their know staff will be able to handle response to the deaths in a professional manner.

ShutDownTheVA@gmail.com

Congress wants more answers about VA campus suicides

A new proposal would require VA to provide lawmakers with information on those veterans' benefits and medical background within days of the deaths.

But that's not true in all cases. A suicide note left by a retired Marine Corps colonel who died by suicide at Bay Pines in December 2018 made clear he had multiple complaints against the department, and earlier this year a veteran killed himself in front of dozens of witnesses in the waiting room of a VA outpatient clinic in Austin, Texas.

About 17 veterans die by suicide each day, according to the latest data released by the department. About four more active-duty, guard and reserve also take their own lives daily. Mandreucci said the department is currently updating the guidance for staff following a suicide on campus, to assist future response and prevention efforts. In addition, "for all events that occur on VA medical facility grounds, VA reviews each event to identify opportunities for further enhancing veteran safety."

That is part of the review still going on at Bay Pines, where officials said they are investigating "to see if changes are warranted" in the wake of the latest death. No timeline has been released for that work.

Veterans experiencing a mental health emergency can contact the Veteran Crisis Line at 1-800-273-8255 and select option 1 for a VA staffer. Veterans, troops or their family

ShutDownTheVA@gmail.com

members can also text 838255 or visit *VeteransCrisisLine.net* for assistance.

About Leo Shane III
Leo covers Congress, Veterans Affairs and the White House for Military Times. He has covered Washington, D.C. since 2004, focusing on military personnel and veterans policies. His work has earned numerous honors, including a 2009 Polk award, a 2010 National Headliner Award, the IAVA Leadership in Journalism award and the VFW News Media award.

ShutDownTheVA@gmail.com

Story #24

2019

VA OIG Response to Suicides by Veterans [35]

The VA just doesn't get it. Veterans are suffering abuse at the hands of their caregivers at the VA. The VA is restricting veterans' constitutional rights by restricting due process rights by denying the right to sue for malpractice.

Incompetence is destroying the quality of their care and misdiagnosis is rampant.

I keep saying this. I don't know why. It seems nobody is listening to the veterans.

You can read this entire summary at:

---

[35]

https://www.google.com/url?sa=t&rct=j&q=&esrc=s&source=web&cd=7&ved=2ahUKEwimydnZzfvlAhVM1VkKHaMwDMUQFjAGegQIARAC&url=https%3A%2F%2Fwww.va.gov%2Foig%2Fpubs%2FVAOIG-19-00501-175.pdf&usg=AOvVaw1nsbwJr_WfHdHop2BFLntt

ShutDownTheVA@gmail.com

https://www.google.com/url?sa=t&rct=j&q=&esrc=s&sour
ce=web&cd=7&ved=2ahUKEwimydnZzfvlAhVM1VkKH
aMwDMUQFjAGegQIARAC&url=https%3A%2F%2Fww
w.va.gov%2Foig%2Fpubs%2FVAOIG-19-00501-
175.pdf&usg=AOvVaw1nsbwJr_WfHdHop2BFLntt

Office of Healthcare Inspections
VETERANS HEALTH ADMINISTRATION

**Alleged Deficiencies in Mental Health Care Prior to a
Death by Suicide at the VA San Diego Healthcare
System California**

HEALTHCARE INSPECTION
REPORT #19-00501-175
AUGUST 7, 2019

In addition to general privacy laws that govern release of
medical information, disclosure of certain veteran health or
other private information may be prohibited by various
federal statutes including, but not limited to, 38 U.S.C.
§§5701, 5705, and 7332, absent an exemption or other
specified circumstances. As mandated by law, the OIG
adheres to privacy and confidentiality laws and regulations
protecting veteran health or other private information in this
report.

Executive Summary

The VA Office of Inspector General (OIG) conducted a
healthcare inspection in response to a hotline complaint
alleging that staff at the San Diego VA Healthcare System
(system), California, failed to provide mental health care to
a patient who subsequently died by suicide. The OIG
identified additional concerns for review including the

ShutDownTheVA@gmail.com

quality of the suicide risk assessment, decision-making process to deactivate the High Risk for Suicide Patient Record Flag (PRF), adequacy of resident supervision, and adequacy of the medication reconciliation process.

The OIG did not substantiate that the system failed to provide mental health care when the patient sought help. The patient first sought care at the system in spring 2017. The patient was referred to mental health services and intermittently engaged in care with an outpatient psychiatrist and outpatient psychologist. The patient engaged in diagnostic testing with a system psychologist and was followed by a suicide prevention coordinator from summer 2017 to spring 2018. When the patient sought mental health services in the emergency department in summer 2018, a psychiatry resident conducted an assessment, and offered medication management and treatment options. The patient declined voluntary inpatient psychiatric admission, expressed feeling safe to go home, and was discharged home with a follow-up care plan. The patient's outpatient psychiatrist attempted to reach the patient by telephone subsequent to the emergency department visit.

The OIG found that the suicide risk assessment of the patient was adequate and complied with Veterans Health Administration (VHA) and system requirements. Upon presenting to the emergency department, the triage nurse immediately assessed for risk of suicide and placed the patient on one-to-one constant observation. The psychiatry resident conducted the required Clinical Suicide Risk Assessment including assessment of firearms access.

ShutDownTheVA@gmail.com

The system complied with VHA and the system's policy regarding resident supervision, supervision documentation, and monitoring of resident supervision documentation. The psychiatry resident documented consultation with the supervisory psychiatrist. The supervisory psychiatrist indicated review and concurrence with the resident provided care through co-signature on the progress note. The system Health Information Management Service demonstrated compliance with quarterly supervision documentation audits, quarterly audits demonstrated meeting the expected compliance rate, and results of audits were reported to the Medical Executive Committee.

The OIG identified deficits in the decision-making process to deactivate the patient's High Risk for Suicide PRF. The assigned Suicide Prevention Coordinator chose to deactivate the patient's High Risk for Suicide PRF in spring 2018 without contacting the patient, without consulting the patient's treatment team, without the patient having any scheduled future appointments, and despite the patient having not been engaged in any mental health services for more than two months. VHA does not have clearly delineated requirements for the decision-making process to deactivate the High Risk for Suicide PRF; however, the Executive Director, Suicide Prevention Program told the OIG that there is an expectation that the suicide prevention coordinator will consult with the patient's treatment team, provide evidence of decreased risk and reduced suicide risk factors, and document rationale for clinical judgment about mental health conditions and behaviors.

The OIG determined that there were deficits in the medication reconciliation process and documentation. Per system policy, the emergency department pharmacist conducted a partial

ShutDownTheVA@gmail.com

medication reconciliation with the patient prior to discharge from the emergency department; however, there was no evidence that the emergency department pharmacist reviewed all medications with the patient and the documentation failed to indicate that the patient self-discontinued two of the active medications on the imported medication list.

The OIG made one recommendation to the Under Secretary for Health related to management of High Risk for Suicide PRFs and one recommendation to the System Director related to the medication reconciliation process and documentation.[11] The recommendation directed to the Under Secretary for Health (USH) was submitted to the Executive in Charge who has the authority to perform the functions and duties of the USH.

Comments

The Executive in Charge, and the Veteran Integrated Service Network and System Directors concurred with the recommendations and provided acceptable action plans. (See appendixes A, B, and C pages 21–25 for the Executive in Charge and Directors' comments.) The OIG considers both recommendations open and will follow up on the planned and recently implemented actions to ensure that they have been effective and sustained.

JOHN D. DAIGH, JR., M.D.
Assistant Inspector General for Healthcare Inspections

ShutDownTheVA@gmail.com

Story #25

When a person experiences severe emotional trauma its difficult to stay calm and rational. That's the point of mental health care treatment, to get help to someone who is having trouble staying calm and rational. And yet, as in the story below, once again, a veteran is dismissed because he is emotional.

My thanks to *USA Today* for allowing me to reprint this story.

2016

Vet set himself on fire after long VA waits, appointment cancellation, investigation finds[36]

Donovan Slack
USA TODAY

---

[36]

https://www.usatoday.com/story/news/politics/2017/11/15/vet-set-himself-fire-after-long-va-waits-appointment-cancellation-investigation-finds/866834001/

ShutDownTheVA@gmail.com

WASHINGTON — A veteran committed suicide by setting himself on fire in front of a New Jersey VA clinic after staff at the clinic repeatedly failed to ensure he received adequate mental health care, an investigation of the death found.

Department of Veterans Affairs staff canceled an appointment Charles Ingram had in fall 2015 because a provider was unavailable, didn't follow up to reschedule, and when he walked into the clinic to ask for an appointment, they didn't schedule it until three months later, the VA inspector general found.

Ingram, a 51-year-old Gulf War veteran, had been approved to receive treatment at a non-VA facility, but no one at VA contacted him or scheduled the appointment.

In March 2016, shortly before his VA appointment, Ingram went to the clinic in Northfield, N.J., doused himself in gasoline and lit himself on fire. The clinic was closed at the time.

"(S)taff failed to follow up on no-shows, clinic cancellations, termination of services, and Non-VA Care Coordination consults as required," the inspector general wrote in a report released Wednesday. "This led to a lack of ordered (mental health) therapy and necessary medications… and may have contributed to his distress."

After the death, VA Secretary David Shulkin allocated more clinical resources to the clinic, removed the hospital director overseeing the facility and directed regional officials to take

ShutDownTheVA@gmail.com

over clinic management. He also instituted same-day mental health services for urgent cases.

But the report provides a tragic glimpse of how appointment-scheduling failures, which have plagued VA facilities across the country for years, can leave veterans desperate and without treatment.

Received mental health care

Ingram had received mental health treatment at the clinic since 2011 but repeatedly had to wait more than a month for appointments. He didn't see a therapist in the year before his death.

When patients go a year without seeing anyone, VA policy dictates that mental health providers reach out to them.

"We found no attempts to follow this process," the inspector general said.

In early 2015, Ingram's VA psychologist asked that he be approved to get outside treatment for neurological impairment. VA administrators approved several therapy sessions. He never got them.

In response to the report, VA officials said schedulers at the Northfield clinic have received more training and new supervisors and managers have been hired. They said regional and local officials also are reorganizing non-VA care coordination.

ShutDownTheVA@gmail.com

"The new structure…ensures high-quality and timely care," wrote Robert Boucher, acting director of the Wilmington VA Medical Center.

Members of Congress from New Jersey, who asked the inspector general to investigate Ingram's death, applauded improvements at the clinic.

"Ingram's death was a tragedy that shook us to the core and reminded us of what's at stake when it comes to providing care for veterans suffering from mental health issues," Sen. Cory Booker, D-N.J., said.

ShutDownTheVA@gmail.com

VA Employees Complained about Veterans

ShutDownTheVA@gmail.com

Story #26

Benjamin Krause is an attorney working to help veterans. And he is good at it. Below is a portion of his website discussing the most insidious practice I have discovered at the Veterans Administration, the blacklisting of veterans by VA employees. Using secret committees, VA employees compile lists of veterans that they feel have not behaved properly (I'm being nice.)

Do I hear Nixon's enemies list?

This is shocking and I thank Mr. Krause for letting me reprint this portion of his website. Please show your appreciation to him by visiting his website at www.disabledveterans.org. You can also sign up for his daily e-mail newsletter.

2014

Illegal VA Complaints Strategy Against Veterans Exposed[37]

By Benjamin Krause August 6, 2014

Last week, journalist Angela Rae exposed despicable treatment of veterans through a little-known process VA employees use against veterans.

Some VA employees illegally lodge VA complaints against veterans to manipulate the purpose of disruptive behavior committees.

Angela Rae interviewed me about how veterans are impacted by this illegal retaliation at the receiving end of VA's disruptive behavior committees.

Disruptive Behavior Committees

Disruptive behavior committees are intended as a catch all to manage hostile and threatening veterans while they seek health care from VA. On the surface, this sounds reasonable. Some veterans are in fact dangerous. However, many nonveterans are also dangerous, and I have yet to see a secret committee like these in civilian hospitals.

My problem with the process is that it is secret. The review process is done in secret and the veteran will not know who sat on the committee or what the evidence presented was prior to the decision. Only after the decision is made are veterans informed of the outcome and given a chance to

---

[37] https://www.disabledveterans.org/2014/08/06/illegal-va-complaints-strategy-against-veterans-exposed/

ShutDownTheVA@gmail.com

appeal the vague allegations. That seems like a due process violation if I have ever seen one.

Further, the process of filing complaints against veterans has been used in many instances where the veteran initially files a complaint against a VA doctor or staff member. In some instances, when a complaint is lodged, VA personnel escalate the intensity of the conversation and even threatening the veteran.

In those instances, VA employees are guilty of illegally filing counter complaints against veterans since the totality of the circumstances would not match the allegations. Unfortunately, VA has a tendency of never believing the veterans, and veteran complaints against VA personnel are almost never received well. As is the case here, in many instances those complaining veterans are instead retaliated against.

I believe this tactic is used to disparage and discredit the veteran when VA reviews the matter.

Background on DC Breakdown Interview

Initially, Angela Rae was outraged when she heard about what VA is doing behind the scenes to retaliate against honest veterans seeking care, so much so that she decided to interview me to learn more about the illegal practice.

It was done via Skype while I was on vacation with family, so the sound has a slight delay. But, you will get a good idea about what is going on and how certain VA doctors and administrators are harming veterans by misusing the process of disruptive behavior committee reviews.

This form of retaliation is, in my opinion, one of the biggest crimes VA is committing across the country because it chills the speech of veterans who respectfully file complaints that have merit. In response to many of these valid complaints, VA employees have been known to file counter complaints that defame the veteran and diminish their credibility. The end result is a veteran having an improper flag on their file, harassment from VA police, and/or restrictions in access to timely health care.

ShutDownTheVA@gmail.com

Cancelled Appointments

ShutDownTheVA@gmail.com

No doubt you heard of a VA hospital in Arizona fiddling around with appointment schedules, secret wait lists and the like and that veterans died because of these antics by VA employees? Let me refresh your memory:

Story #27

PHOENIX VA APPOINTMENT CANCELATION

VA Office of Inspector General Releases Phoenix Consult Mismanagement Report[38]

Some Consults Inappropriately Discontinued Because of Unclear Procedures

WASHINGTON – The VA Office of Inspector General (VA OIG) today issued its report, Review of Alleged Consult

---

[38] https://www.va.gov/oig/pubs/press-releases/VAOIG-PhoenixConsultsNewsRelease.pdf

ShutDownTheVA@gmail.com

Mismanagement at the Phoenix VA Health Care System, which substantiated that the Phoenix VA Health Care System (PVAHCS) inappropriately discontinued consults for patients. The OIG initiated the review to look into allegations made in 2015 by a confidential complainant and reported to the OIG by the House Committee on Veterans' Affairs.

"Because consults were inappropriately discontinued, some patients did not receive the care requested or experienced delays in receiving care," said Michael J. Missal, Inspector General, U.S. Department of Veterans Affairs Office of Inspector General. "OIG's 14 recommendations will help improve consult procedures at PVAHCS and ensure veterans receive the follow-up medical care with specialty doctors that they earned through their service in our military."

The OIG's review found that during calendar year 2015, PVAHCS staff inappropriately discontinued and canceled consults, and were generally unclear about following specific consult management procedures. Procedures and consult management responsibilities varied in different specialties throughout the system, which further led to staff confusion and, in some cases, canceling consults.

In August 2014, the OIG reported on numerous allegations regarding patient deaths, patient wait times, and scheduling practices at PVAHCS. That report recommended that the VA Secretary ensure PVAHCS follow VA consult guidance and appropriately review consults before closing them to ensure veterans receive necessary medical care. Although VHA made efforts to improve the care provided at PVAHCS,

ShutDownTheVA@gmail.com

the OIG found that consult management issues remained almost a year later.

The OIG conducts oversight of VA and its programs and operations, providing independent and objective reporting to the VA Secretary and the Congress for the purpose of preventing and detecting fraud and abuse, and bringing about positive change in the integrity, efficiency, and effectiveness of VA. To report potential criminal activity, fraud, waste, mismanagement, or other abuse, contact the VA OIG Hotline at vaoighotline@va.gov or www.va.gov/oig/hotline/default.asp.

The Rest of the Story

Did you know this was not the first time VA employees screwed veterans by cancelling their appointments?

Read on.

ShutDownTheVA@gmail.com

Story #28

My thanks to the Florida Times-Union of Jacksonville, Florida for permission to reprint their story below.

2015

Jacksonville VA canceled nearly 60,000 veterans' health appointments in 14-month span[39]

By Clifford Davis, Florida Times-Union Jacksonville, FL
Posted Apr 3, 2015 at 5:46 PM

In February, the assistant director of the North Florida/South Georgia VA Health System pointed to canceled appointments as a contributing factor in the Jacksonville clinic's wait times, which are the worst for any major VA facility in the country.

What Nick Ross failed to mention was that the clinic - not patients - was responsible for canceling more than half of those appointments.

---

[39] https://www.jacksonville.com/article/20150403/NEWS/801242469

ShutDownTheVA@gmail.com

"We have a fairly high number of folks who either cancel their appointment or no-show, this accounting system really doesn't take that into effect because it's cumulative," Ross said when presented with Jacksonville's wait times. Then, as now, roughly a quarter of veterans at the Jacksonville clinic don't get seen within the VA's 30-day target, more than seven percent higher any other major facility in the nation. "If you take that into account, technically speaking, we can't do anything about that."

The numbers tell another story.

Out of 117,117 canceled appointments from Jan 1, 2014, to March 1, 2015, the clinic canceled 59,661 of them, according to data provided by the VA through a Freedom of Information Act request made by the Times-Union.

The cancelations are important because they add to already lengthy waits for veterans attempting to get healthcare. Patient wait times, and some VA administrators' attempts to cover them up to receive bonuses, were the paramount issue in the VA scandal that erupted in Phoenix last year - eventually leading to VA secretary Eric Shinseki's resignation.

In Northeast Florida, Jacksonville, as mentioned, is last in the nation among major facilities for wait times.

In St. Augustine, the VA's lack of action in finding a new home for the clinic there will cost taxpayers at least hundreds of thousands of dollars.

ShutDownTheVA@gmail.com

In Gainesville, a recently released inspector general report found nepotism and preferential treatment there.

All three facilities are managed by the North Florida/South Georgia VA Health System.

During the 14-month period, the clinic scheduled 627,078 appointments. Nearly 10 percent of them were canceled by the clinic.

The VA cited reasons why appointments are canceled.

"Any change in provider ... requires cancellation of patient appointments and rescheduling," wrote area VA spokeswoman Cindy Snook in an emailed statement. "We schedule patient appointments 120 days into the future.

"Any associated appointments such as lab, X-ray, etc. would also require cancellation and rescheduling."

If a provider is sick or on leave, that would also require an appointment to be canceled, Snook said.

Still, the Jacksonville clinic's cancellation rate dwarfs those at other similar-sized clinics in the state.

In a February interview with the Times-Union, Ross cited the cancellation rate as a reason why wait times at the Jacksonville facility were so much longer than other clinics in the state that have fewer physicians per appointments.

ShutDownTheVA@gmail.com

No one associated with the Jacksonville clinic or its leadership was available Friday to say why Jacksonville's rate was so much higher.

The Times-Union requested the statistics after numerous patients detailed how their appointment dates were changed or canceled - many times without their knowledge.

"Sometimes you go to the VA appointment and they'll say you're appointment has been canceled, you have to come back on another day," said Tony D'Aleo, a veteran and president of the Jacksonville chapter of Vietnam Veterans of America. "I would never cancel them.

"The VA canceled them."

Russ Jones received a letter in the mail, dated Feb. 24, 2015, from the VA notifying him of an appointment with a podiatrist March 30 - outside the VA's target of 30 days, though just barely.

Ten days before the appointment, he was sent a letter in the mail notifying him the Jacksonville clinic had cancelled his appointment.

"We apologize for the inconvenience," the letter said, though it gave no reason as to why. "Your appointment will be rescheduled as soon as possible."

You can read more articles from the Jacksonville, Florida Times-Union at www.jacksonville.com

Story #29

This story comes from the Washington Free Beacon. Thank you for allowing the reprint of your story. Please visit The Washington Free Beacon at www.freebeacon.com.

2006

Houston Veterans Waited for Care After VA Cancelled Appointments[40]

Evidence that VA hospital was falsifying records as recently as February

AP Morgan Chalfant - June 22, 2016 3:45 PM
Nearly 100 veterans in Houston waited an average of 81 days for care after schedulers at a Department of Veterans Affairs hospital cancelled their appointments, a watchdog said this week.

---

[40] https://freebeacon.com/issues/houston-vets-waited-for-care-after-cancelled-appointments/

ShutDownTheVA@gmail.com

The veterans' wait times appeared much shorter in electronic scheduling records because staffers at the Michael E. DeBakey Medical Center in Houston, Texas were told to designate appointments as cancelled by the patient when they were really cancelled by the facility, according to a VA inspector general report released on Monday.

Investigators learned through a review that two former scheduling supervisors at the hospital and a current director of two of its outpatient clinics told staffers as recently as February to designate appointments cancelled by the clinic as cancelled by patients.

"This report is a prime example of why VA is still mired in dysfunction. The inspector general caught three VA leaders red-handed instructing their subordinates to manipulate wait times," Rep. Jeff Miller (R., Fla.), who chairs the House Committee on Veterans Affairs, told the *Washington Free Beacon.*

Miller said one of the VA leaders was allowed to retire with full benefits, while the other two still work at the VA.

The watchdog launched an investigation into the medical center after an anonymous tip that leaders were instructing staffers at the hospital and its outpatient clinics to incorrectly record appointments.

The inspector general found that, between July 2014 and June 2015, 223 out of 373 appointments designated as cancelled by the patient in electronic hospital records were in fact cancelled by hospital staffers.

ShutDownTheVA@gmail.com

Because the VA measures wait times differently for appointments rescheduled due to clinic cancellations and those rescheduled due to patient cancellations, the action caused nearly 100 veterans' wait times to be grossly understated in electronic records.

When the clinic cancels a patient's appointment, the wait time is still calculated from the original clinically-indicated or preferred appointment date. When a patient cancels an appointment, the VA resets the preferred appointment date to the patient's new preferred date.

Of the 223 falsely designated appointments, 94 were rescheduled beyond the VA's 30-day wait goal.

These veterans waited an average of 81 days—almost three months—for care, though the hospital's electronic records showed they waited an average of three days for care.

Investigators also found evidence that staffers did not always use the correct date when scheduling veterans' appointments, which resulted in waits being understated. The electronic records for 50 appointments understated wait times by 66 days on average. Thirty-eight of these records falsely indicated that veterans waited zero days for appointments.

The Houston VA was one of 112 facilities flagged by the Veterans Health Administration in a system-wide review because of concerns over inappropriate scheduling practices in 2014, after hospital staffers at the Phoenix VA were found keeping secret lists to hide long waits for care. According to findings of that investigation released in March, the watchdog found evidence that Houston VA employees were "zeroing out" wait times by basing preferred appointment dates on available clinic appointments.

"These conditions persisted because of lack of effective training and oversight. As a result, [Veterans Health Administration] recorded wait times did not reflect the actual wait experienced by the veterans and the wait time remained unreliable and understated," the inspector general wrote in the report released Monday.

The watchdog recommended that VA management confer with the agency's Office of Accountability Review to decide whether any administrative action should be taken. The inspector general also urged managers to provide staff with better training in scheduling procedures and audit scheduling practices.

A spokesman for the Houston VA told the *Washington Free Beacon* that the medical center started retraining employees in scheduling practices two years ago and has implemented monthly audits of scheduled appointments.

"We are confident that our dedicated schedulers (46 percent of whom are Veterans themselves) now clearly understand the procedures related to scheduling Veterans for appointments," Maureen Dyman, the medical center's communications director, said in an emailed statement.

ShutDownTheVA@gmail.com

Dyman said the investigation "did not substantiate any case of Houston VA Medical Center senior leaders intentionally manipulating scheduling data."

A representative for Concerned Veterans for America, a veterans group advocating for VA reform, said the report "shows that veterans are still at the mercy of ethically challenged VA officials."

"Instructing staff to incorrectly record cancellations is proof-positive of the VA's desire to avoid accountability for its failure to deliver timely care," said Cody McGregor, the group's national outreach director and a former U.S. Army sniper. "The corruption and complete disregard inside the VA towards the men and women who sacrificed everything for our country is shameful."

The VA has been criticized by lawmakers and some groups who say the agency has not done enough to reduce veterans' wait times and punish its employees for misconduct. Last week, VA officials said they would no longer use streamlined firing powers to punish employees for misconduct because of pending legal challenges.

"We are holding people accountable," VA Secretary Robert McDonald said about the decision during a Monday talk at the Brookings Institution. "We have taken advantage of accelerated process for nine senior executive service individuals. What we decided recently is, given that that part of the law has come under constitutional question, we didn't want to continue to follow that procedure since what we don't want to do is have a disciplinary process go on and then have it overturned later for a technicality."

"We are using the old procedure. The old procedure is fine," McDonald added.

McDonald came under fire earlier this year for comparing veterans' waits for care to lines for Disney theme park rides and suggesting wait times are not the best metric of success for the agency. He has since expressed regret for those statements.

Morgan Chalfant is a staff writer at the Washington Free Beacon. Prior to joining the Free Beacon, Morgan worked as a staff writer at Red Alert Politics. She also served as the year-long Collegiate Network fellow on the editorial page at USA TODAY from 2013-14. Morgan graduated from Boston College in 2013 with a B.A. in English and Mathematics. Her Twitter handle is @mchalfant16.

ShutDownTheVA@gmail.com

Story #30

2018

'I knew something was not right': Mass cancellations of diagnostic test orders at VA hospitals draw scrutiny[41]

Thank you to USA Today for allowing the reprint of this article. And kudos to Donovan Slack for her incredible reporting on veterans affairs..

Donovan Slack, USA TODAY
IOWA CITY, Iowa – Radiology technologist Jeff Dettbarn said he knew something was wrong at the Department of Veterans Affairs hospital in Iowa City, Iowa, when a patient arrived in February 2017 for a CT scan, but the doctor's order for it had been canceled.

---

[41]

https://www.usatoday.com/story/news/politics/2018/10/01/va-hospitals-cancellations-diagnostic-exam-orders-draw-scrutiny/1424298002/

ShutDownTheVA@gmail.com

"To have a patient show up for a scan and not have an order – you're like, 'What the heck is going on?' " he told USA TODAY in an interview.

Dettbarn started collecting cancellation notices for diagnostic procedures such as CT scans, MRIs and ultrasounds.

"I knew something was not right," he said. "Because none of them were canceled by a physician."

Cancellations of more than 250,000 radiology orders at VA hospitals across the country since 2016 have raised questions about whether – in a rush to clear out outdated and duplicate diagnostic orders – some facilities failed to follow correct procedures. At issue is a concern over whether some medically necessary orders for CT scans and other imaging tests were canceled improperly.

The VA inspector general is auditing mass cancellations at eight VA medical centers "to determine whether VA processed radiology requests in a timely manner and appropriately managed canceled requests," VA Inspector General Michael Missal said.

Those hospitals are in Tampa and Bay Pines, Florida; Salisbury, North Carolina; Cleveland; Dallas; Denver; Las Vegas; and Los Angeles.

After receiving inquiries from USA TODAY, a ninth was added – Iowa City.

In Iowa City, Dettbarn alerted the hospital's compliance officer about his concerns. He is now facing disciplinary proceedings and contends they are an effort to retaliate against him.

The VA declined to comment on disciplinary proceedings without Dettbarn's written consent to discuss personnel matters, which he did not provide.

This much is clear: in sworn testimony in the disciplinary proceedings against Dettbarn, Iowa City administrative staffer Lisa Bickford saidshe and other employees were told by the hospital's chief radiologist that they needed to "clean" up a backlog of incomplete diagnostic orders, some dating back years.

The staff responded by "annihilating" thousands of orders in a matter of weeks, Bickford said.

Failure to Follow Guidelines
Bryan Clark, a spokesman for the Iowa City hospital, acknowledged the facility failed to follow national VA guidelines for diagnostic order cancellations but said that happened in only a "small number of instances" and "anything closed improperly was reviewed" and actions were taken to try to ensure veterans received any needed exams. He said the process was intended to "ensure the quality and safety of the care delivered to veteran patients."

The VA said many of the orders were outdated or duplicated. The agency said it welcomes the oversight and is working with the inspector general to improve cancellation guidelines.

ShutDownTheVA@gmail.com

VA officials said efforts to close the loop on test orders with physicians and veterans surpass private-sector practices.
Laurence Meyer, the chief doctor overseeing specialty care for the national VA, told USA TODAY he didn't want to comment on how individual VA hospitals handled cancellations, but he acknowledged "we've received word that a few places haven't been following the directive as intended."

"We've sent out teams and have reviewed and are aggressively working to fix that," he said.

The VA's guidelines on order cancellations have undergone revisions in the past few years.

In 2016, hospitals were told to try contacting patients multiple times before cancellations. Last year, the rules required review by a radiologist or the ordering provider before canceling. If the tests were still needed, patients should be contacted to schedule them. Since last year, hospitals have been required to establish a fail-safe "triage" process, such as written verification of review by providers.

Concerns about diagnostic test order cancellations have also been raised at the VA hospital in Tampa. Employees estimated they canceled thousands of radiology orders without checking first with doctors or patients, according to depositions in a discrimination lawsuit brought by four ultrasound technicians.

ShutDownTheVA@gmail.com

Those technicians told USA TODAY they worry veterans may have gone months, if not a year or longer, before they or their doctors realized tests weren't performed – if they realized at all. Technologist Erin Tonkyro noted that risk factors for many veterans are higher than for other patients. "Cancer grows very quickly, and our patients are not like those patients on the outside – it doesn't mean that cancer doesn't happen in private practice. But our veterans have been exposed to such a large amount of toxic environments like Agent Orange; now we're talking about the burn pits that have happened overseas," Tonkyro said.

'We knew it was bad'

At the Tampa facility, radiology managers began tackling outstanding orders in fall 2016.

As many as 10 people were tasked with the job, one administrative staffer testified in a deposition in the technicians' lawsuit. Multiple employees testified they canceled orders by date and did not consult any doctors before doing so, nor was there patient contact.

They disabled office printers because of the volume of cancellations – one employee estimated they canceled thousands of radiology orders, according to testimony.

"That's when we really started getting worried," said Tonkyro, who attended the depositions with her co-plaintiffs, ultrasound technologists Yenny Hernandez, Kara Mitchell-Davis and Dana Strauser. "We knew it was bad, but we had no idea the magnitude of how bad it was."

ShutDownTheVA@gmail.com

Strauser told USA TODAY that administrators went beyond past orders and canceled future ones. Those could have been follow-up scans for veterans who might have been at risk of developing medical conditions, such as cancer recurrence.

"Doctors will put an order in for six months in advance and sometimes even a year in advance, and we were getting cancellations of those future orders," she said.

In a statement issued by VA spokesman Curt Cashour, the VA declined to comment on what happened in Tampa, citing the litigation. "However, we are confident the James A. Haley Veterans' Hospital has processes and procedures in place to provide the best care possible for our patients," the statement said.

The Tampa Bay Times first reported the technicians' concerns in July, and the hospital's chief of staff, Colleen Jakey, wrote to providers the following month asking them to review canceled orders, according to a copy of the correspondence obtained by USA TODAY.

"We believe appropriate action was taken," Jakey wrote, adding that a review of a random sample of cancellations did not turn up any cases of harm to veterans. "This is a second-level review of these orders to confirm that each of these patients received the appropriate care and/or follow up."

The technicians told USA TODAY some doctors have since reordered canceled exams but won't know whether veteran patients suffered any harm from the delays until they are performed and assessed.

ShutDownTheVA@gmail.com

'An important patient safety issue'

VA hospitals came under increasing pressure to address outstanding diagnostic orders after a conference call that national officials convened with radiology managers across the country in January 2017. More than 325,000 orders for scans of veteran patients had not been completed nationwide.

The VA's top radiologist, Robert Sherrier, called it "an important patient safety issue" in a presentation for the call. "Ordered studies are not being performed on veterans, and providers may not be aware that the ordered study has not been completed," he said.

In a dozen states, there were VA medical centers with more than 5,000 outstanding orders, his presentation said. The numbers reached 29,000 in Columbia, S.C.; 21,000 in Cleveland; and 12,000 in Washington.

ShutDownTheVA@gmail.com

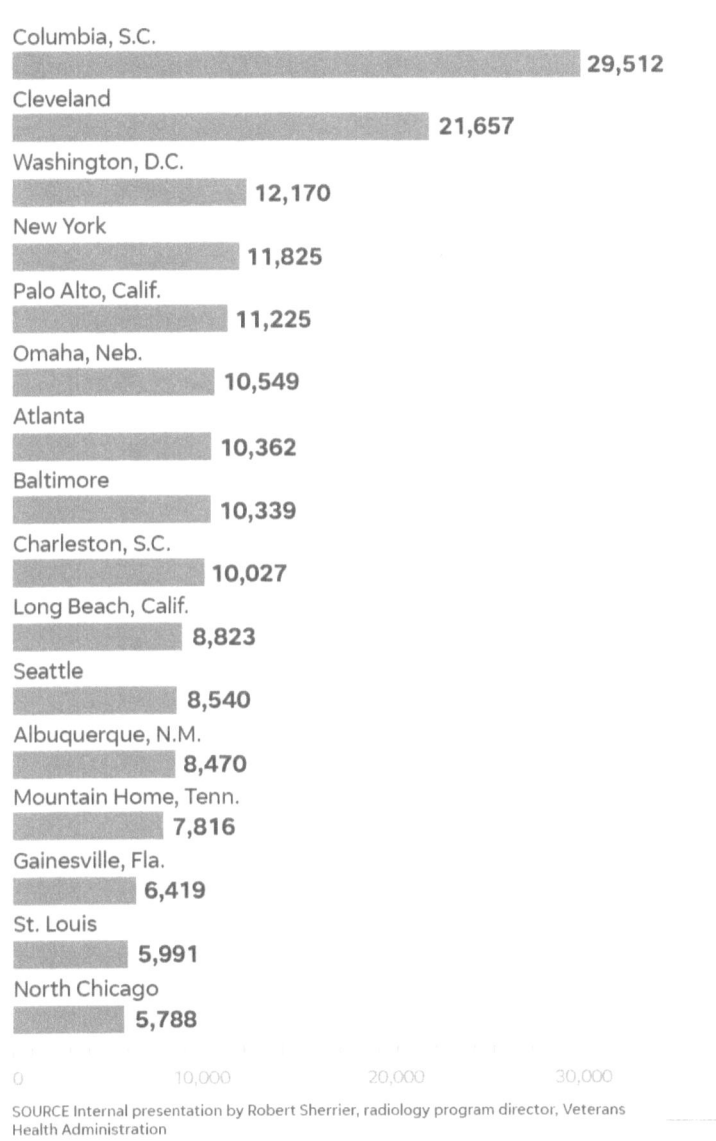

**Outstanding radiology orders
at VA hospitals in January 2017**

Columbia, S.C. — 29,512

Cleveland — 21,657

Washington, D.C. — 12,170

New York — 11,825

Palo Alto, Calif. — 11,225

Omaha, Neb. — 10,549

Atlanta — 10,362

Baltimore — 10,339

Charleston, S.C. — 10,027

Long Beach, Calif. — 8,823

Seattle — 8,540

Albuquerque, N.M. — 8,470

Mountain Home, Tenn. — 7,816

Gainesville, Fla. — 6,419

St. Louis — 5,991

North Chicago — 5,788

0   10,000   20,000   30,000

SOURCE Internal presentation by Robert Sherrier, radiology program director, Veterans Health Administration
Frank Pompa/USA TODAY

Some dated back to the 1980s, but others were only months old. VA officials said that in some cases, staff may not have been able to contact veterans to schedule exams. In other cases, veterans may not have shown up, possibly because their ailments had gone away. Some orders may have been duplicates ordered by two different doctors.

Others may have been tests that were still needed – to monitor tumors or follow up on emergency room visits, for example.

A panel of medical and ethics specialists conducted thousands of chart reviews, Meyer said, and determined orders for exams due to be performed before June 2015 could be canceled outright without jeopardizing veteran health.

Orders due after that date required further steps to ensure patient safety.

The national call to action triggered a dramatic reduction in pending exam orders overdue by two months or longer. As of last month, the VA said, there were 31,000 nationwide.

'We look terrible'
At the Iowa City VA hospital, Bickford said the chief of radiology – who also was the top radiology official in the Midwest for the VA – told her after the conference call in January 2017 that the facility had more outstanding orders than any other VA in the region.

"He came to (us) and said, 'We've got to get this cleaned up now. I mean, we look terrible,' " Bickford said. So she and other staff "went through and started annihilating orders," she testified in the disciplinary proceeding against Dettbarn. Any radiology orders more than 60 days past due were considered "invalid" and "expired," Bickford testified. That is at odds with VA guidelines at the time requiring doctor reviews.

Cancellation records reviewed by USA TODAY show that in some instances, she and other staff canceled future orders. In one case, a nurse practitioner ordered an ultrasound for September 2017 as a six-month follow-up for a veteran with a history of kidney stones. An X-ray technician canceled it in June 2017, calling it an "expired" order.

That same month, records indicate, Bickford canceled an order for a follow-up CT scan to monitor a veteran's lung nodules. The test wasn't due to be performed until September 2017. Also in June, she canceled a CT to monitor fluid in a patient's lung not due until November 2017. Records show Bickford selected "patient failed to contact clinic" in both cases. None of the records reviewed by USA TODAY contained personal information identifying patients.

Discipline
In the disciplinary case against Dettbarn, his supervisors alleged he was "disruptive" and didn't send one patient's images to be interpreted – accusations he denied. The investigation was initiated soon after he reported his concerns about the order cancellations.

ShutDownTheVA@gmail.com

The Office of Special Counsel, a federal agency tasked with protecting whistle-blowers, is investigating, according to a letter from the office.

Bickford declined to comment and referred questions to the Iowa City VA. In her sworn testimony, she blamed scheduling clerks for not indicating on orders that exams were scheduled. That led employees to assume there was a "dead order" even though a patient had a future appointment, she said, but she estimated that occurred only "maybe a half a dozen times." When patients arrived for appointments, the errors were discovered, new orders were created and the exams went ahead, she said.

The chief of radiology, Stanley Parker, did not respond to a message seeking comment at a number listed in public records. In his deposition in the case, he testified that he believed physician-review would have been done before canceling.

Clark, the hospital spokesman, said Bickford's testimony about "annihilating" orders was not in context and referred to the "success of the process to right size the number" of outstanding radiology orders at the hospital.

Clark said he doesn't know how many orders were canceled at the facility because officials didn't track it, but he said more than 4,000 were canceled in January and February 2017 in the southern part of the Midwest region.

Clark said "most" canceled orders were from before 2015, though he didn't know how many. He said "some" exam orders were "canceled without following proper policies or procedures."

In those instances, Clark said, "appropriate personnel actions were taken to correct the behavior, and staff reviewed the cancellations to ensure every order that required action was appropriately reviewed by a radiology provider."

Dettbarn has been detailed to a job collating VA records since July 2017. He said that whatever happens to him, he wants the public to know about what he called a "horrible shortcut" administrators took to improve the numbers. Dettbarn said Iowa City officials should do a clinical review like the Tampa VA to ensure veterans weren't harmed.

"It's so far beyond wrong what was done," he said. "This is someone's health care, this is their body, their life you're screwing with, and people are playing doctor that aren't physicians."

Contributing: Tony Leys, The Des Moines Register

ShutDownTheVA@gmail.com

Story #31

2019

VA closes facilities, cancels appointments in three states as the agency braces for Dorian[42]

Thanks to Stars and Stripes for allowing the reprint of this article.

By NIKKI WENTLING **AND** ROSE L. THAYER |
STARS AND STRIPES Published: September 3, 2019

The Department of Veterans Affairs on Tuesday braced for the effects of Hurricane Dorian by closing health care facilities and canceling appointments in three states as the slow-moving storm creeped closer to the U.S. East Coast.

---

[42] https://www.stripes.com/news/veterans/va-closes-facilities-cancels-appointments-in-three-states-as-the-agency-braces-for-dorian-1.597121

ShutDownTheVA@gmail.com

The agency ordered dozens of VA outpatient clinics across Florida, Georgia and South Carolina closed Tuesday.

The VA hospital in Miami and the Bay Pines VA Healthcare System near Tampa, Fla., were closed Tuesday but planned to be fully operational Wednesday as Dorian was predicted to move farther north.

VA health care facilities were expected to remain closed Wednesday along the East Coast of Florida and the south-central portion of the state, including Daytona Beach, Viera, Deltona, Moore Haven and Clewiston.

Related Articles
The West Palm Beach VA Medical Center was operating Tuesday on a limited basis, treating only existing patients and emergencies. It was unclear Tuesday when the facility would resume all operations.

In Georgia, mandatory evacuations of Glynn County in the southeastern part of the state led to the closure of one VA health care facility in Brunswick on Tuesday and Wednesday.

Six VA health care clinics in South Carolina, as well as the Ralph H. Johnson VA Medical Center in Charleston, cancelled veterans' appointments scheduled for Tuesday through Saturday.

According to the National Hurricane Center, Dorian's effects are predicted to be felt along the coasts of Florida, Georgia and South Carolina from Tuesday through Thursday.

ShutDownTheVA@gmail.com

As of Tuesday afternoon, it was designated a Category 2 hurricane, meaning there's potential for extensive damage caused by extremely dangerous winds.

The VA established a disaster line for veterans in the area affected by Dorian. Veterans and their families can call 1-800-507-4571 to learn where to go for care and how to receive prescription drugs, as well as to ask any other questions.

wentling.nikki@stripes.com   ***Twitter:****@nikkiwentling*
thayer.rose@stripes.com   ***Twitter:*** *@Rose_Lori*

Story #32

2019

Investigation: Mass cancellations of diagnostic test orders at VA hospitals draw scrutiny[43]

Thousands of medical tests delayed, improperly canceled at VA facilities, audit finds

Thanks to USA Today for allowing the reprint of this article. www.usatoday.com

Donovan Slack USA TODAY

WASHINGTON – Veterans Affairs employees improperly canceled tens of thousands of orders for diagnostic medical tests such as X-rays and cardiac imaging, jeopardizing the health of some patients, a wide-ranging audit by the VA's inspector general found.

In other cases, tests were delayed for weeks.

---

[43] https://www.usatoday.com/story/news/nation/2019/12/11/thousands-veteran-medical-tests-delayed-improperly-canceled-va/4387520002/

ShutDownTheVA@gmail.com

Auditors blamed the problems on backlogs, breakdowns and mismanagement at every level, from the facilities around the country where veterans get medical care to headquarters in Washington, D.C.

In one case outlined by auditors, a veteran waited 42 days for an MRI after a CT scan detected a lesion in his brain. Urgent tests like that should be done within two weeks.

The patient's test was not scheduled until a doctor called, more than a month after ordering the test, to ask why it hadn't been done.

The test result "identified a type of malformation that can cause brain hemorrhages," the audit said. It didn't identify the facility where the delay occurred.

The audit, released Tuesday, corroborates a USA TODAY investigation last year that revealed more than 250,000 radiology orders at VA hospitals across the country had been canceled since 2016.

Mass cancellations
After reviewing exam orders at VA facilities in several states, auditors concluded staff did not follow guidelines when canceling an estimated 106,000 requests for radiology and nuclear medicine tests. That meant tests were delayed or may not have been done.

The cancellations occurred from September through December 2017, but many of the tests had been ordered months or years earlier.

Radiology supervisors didn't have controls "to ensure canceled ... requests received the appropriate clinical review," auditors wrote.

Auditors did not conclude veterans had been harmed, but they found lapses that put them at risk.

The VA's inspector general referred a half-dozen cases, out of a sampling of 113 canceled orders, to VA officials for further review because those patients may still need the diagnostics.

They included an ultrasound exam of a veteran's liver ordered in 2016, a CT scan of a vet's chest requested in 2017, a kidney ultrasound order from 2017 and an aortic ultrasound requested in 2015.

VA pledges improvement
VA officials acknowledged the problems and pledged to make changes. That includes ensuring those veterans get any needed care they didn't receive.

"Our office has expended considerable resources and time to develop solutions to the concerns raised," the national VA radiology office said in a written response to the audit.

USA TODAY's report raised questions about whether some facilities, in an effort to clear out outdated or duplicate diagnostic orders, canceled orders that veterans may still have needed.

ShutDownTheVA@gmail.com

The Peter Principle

ShutDownTheVA@gmail.com

The **Peter Principle** is a theory originated by Dr. Laurence J. Peter. It states that successful members of a <u>hierarchical organization</u> are eventually promoted to their highest level of <u>competence</u>, after which further promotion raises them to a level at which they are not competent. The term is a pun on <u>Sigmund Freud</u>'s theory of the pleasure principle.[44]

This next story is a perfect example of how difficult it is to get rid of employees who are career bureaucrats. The system protects them. The system promotes them. Think of it as The Peter Principle on Steroids. Read on.

[44] https://psychology.wikia.org/wiki/Peter_principle

ShutDownTheVA@gmail.com

Story #33

2014

Drugs, corruption go unpunished in Mississippi VA center[45]

This story reprinted with the kind permission of the dailycaller.com. Please visit their website for more fascinating stories. While you're there, thank them for helping keep America informed. www.dailycaller.com

Michael Volpe Contributor   March 19, 2014 7:29 PM ET

A number of top level managers at the G.V. (Sonny) Montgomery Veterans Administration Medical Center in Jackson, Miss. remain employed in their positions or in other positions within the Veterans Administration despite an Office of Special Counsel report from 2013 that implicated each in criminal wrongdoing, The Daily Caller has learned.

---

[45] https://dailycaller.com/2014/03/19/drugs-corruption-go-unpunished-in-mississippi-va-center/
https://dailycaller.com/2014/03/19/drugs-corruption-go-unpunished-in-mississippi-va-center/

A 22-page letter from Office of Special Counsel (OSC) investigator Carolyn Lerner from September 13, 2013 implicated several members in the criminal wrongdoing: Joe Battle, the director of the Sonny Montgomery Medical Center; Dr. Kent Kirchner, the chief operating officer; Dr. James Lockyer, the head of Primary Care; and Dorothy White-Taylor, the former associate director of patient care. The letter, addressed to President Barack Obama, also implicated Dr. Gregg Parker, the chief medical officer for Veteran Integration Services Network 16, which oversees a basket of hospitals including the Sonny Montgomery Medical Center.

The report stated that many of the problems stemmed from the hospital's reliance on nurse practitioners at the expense of doctors, largely at the behest of Dorothy White-Taylor.

According to the report, there were "numerous issues regarding patient safety, provision of services, and certification of medical providers." Specifically, Drs. Kirchner and Lockyer were implicated in the report for prescribing medication to patients they didn't treat.

"Dr. Kirchner and Dr. Lockyer commonly signed the form [to prescribe narcotics] as the certifying physician even though providing patient care was never a part of their duties."

The report also implicated Battle and Dr. Parker for pressuring doctors at the Sonny Montgomery Medical Center to sign a collaborative agreement with nurse practitioners (NPs), even though the doctors weren't in a

ShutDownTheVA@gmail.com

position to supervise the NPs, and could be subject to malpractice suits if the NPs committed a medical error. According to the report, when some doctors resisted signing these collaborative agreements, Battle and Dr. Parker threatened to withhold part of their paychecks.

Additionally, the report cited a series of emails from Dorothy "Dot" Taylor-White to medical staff encouraging doctors to sign off for narcotics prescriptions for patients seen by NPs, a criminal act according to one of the whistleblowers, Dr. Phyllis Hollenbeck. The report further stated that Taylor's power and clout in the hospital caused doctors to be fearful of reporting this misdeeds.

"Dr. Hollenbeck further stated physicians were ignored when they raised concerns about NPs practicing as [licensed independent practitioners] LIPs, because NPs and Ms. White-Taylor had significant power in the facility, such that physicians feared retaliation," the report reads.

The problems at the Sonny Montgomery Medical Center have been the subject of two House Veteran Affairs Committee (HVAC) hearings, in September and November 2013, along with the OSC report. Despite all this oversight, no one has been held to account, said whistleblowers Dr. Hollenbeck and Erik Heaton, a military veteran who served for more than 40 years.

Battle continues to be the director of the Sonny Montgomery Medical Center. Dr. Lockyer was transferred to the Mountain Home, Tennessee VA Medical Center, where he is currently a physician. Dr. Parker continues to be the chief

ShutDownTheVA@gmail.com

medical officer of the region. Only Dot Taylor is no longer with the VA system.

Taylor was arrested on drug charges in early 2012, before the events in the OSC report, only to have those charges dropped in March 2013. Taylor was working in a managerial role at the Veterans Integrated Service Network (VISN) regional office until she retired on March 7, 2014, and her final salary was $163,574, according to VISN 16 public affairs officer Benita McClellan.

A phone call and email to the media department at the VA wasn't returned, and an email to VA Secretary General Eric Shinseki was also not answered.

In the September 2013 HVAC hearing, VISN 16 Director Rica Lewis-Payton, who oversees the Sonny Montgomery Medical Center, defended the region and stressed that accountability was a priority.

"Be assured that we have thoroughly investigated various allegations," Lewis-Payton said. "We know that a number of issues have been raised about this center, and we take those concerns seriously. We work aggressively to identify and correct any errors, and we are adopting a series of significant reforms to improve the center. When appropriate to do so, we hold people accountable."

UPDATE:
The V.A. responded to The DC's request for comment after this article was published, writing:

ShutDownTheVA@gmail.com

V.A. is deeply committed to providing the quality care and benefits our nation's veterans have earned and deserve. V.A. welcomes recommendations of the Office of Special Counsel as an opportunity to evaluate our programs and identify areas for improvement. Although the Office of Special Counsel review team determined that no changes in agency rules, regulations, or practices should be made as a result of this investigation, the fact-finding team made a number of recommendations for the facility to adhere to or enforce current rules, regulations, practices and policies. Leadership from the G.V. (Sonny) Montgomery V.A. Medical Center has developed an action plan and monitors responsibilities for each of the recommended actions described in the report.

V.A. takes seriously any issue that occurs at one of the more than 1,800 facilities across the country. All employees are expected to help V.A. achieve its mission of providing veterans the highest quality care possible. When an incident occurs, V.H.A. [Veterans Health Administration] leadership conducts a prompt review to understand what happened, prevent similar incidents in the future, hold those responsible accountable consistent with due process under the law, and share lessons learned across the system.

Next up…

What happened to the employees in this story responsible for the deaths of veterans? Fired? Reprimanded? How about rewarded?

Read on.

ShutDownTheVA@gmail.com

Rewarding Murder

ShutDownTheVA@gmail.com

Story #34

2016

Exclusive: VA shuffles managers, declares 'new leadership'[46]

Reprinted with permission of USATODAY. Thank you for taking care of veterans, those who serve to protect you. www.usatoday.com

WASHINGTON — Although Veterans Affairs Secretary Bob McDonald has asserted that more than "90%" of the VA's medical centers have "new leadership" or "leadership teams" since he took over the troubled agency in 2014, a USA TODAY investigation found the VA has hired just eight medical center directors from outside the agency during that time.

---

[46]

https://www.usatoday.com/story/news/politics/2016/10/18/veterans-affairs-managers-transfer-new-leadership-medical-centers/91965888/

ShutDownTheVA@gmail.com

The rest of the "new leadership" McDonald cites is the result of moving existing managers between jobs and medical centers. Some managers were transferred to new jobs despite concerns about the care provided to veterans at the facilities they were previously managing.

USA TODAY determined that of 140 medical center directors, 92 are new since McDonald took office in July 2014. That's 66%. Of those, only 69 are permanent placements; the rest are interim appointees. And all but eight of these directors already worked at the VA.

11/25/2019 4:58 p.m.

VA officials said McDonald cited an erroneous statistic and the actual percentage of new medical center leaders is 84%. That figure includes new chiefs of staff, associate directors and other top executives, even where center directors remained the same. The agency considers a center as having new leadership if one member of its top management team has transferred from another center or job.

"I said very carefully, and I've always said 'leadership or leadership teams' — both are important," McDonald said in an interview. "In some cases, you've got directors who are doing a great job, but they've got a chief of staff who's not and you've got to change that person."

McDonald said the number itself is "almost irrelevant" and what's important is that he and other VA leaders are "trying to attract top talent, to get them in the right seats on the bus, in order to make outcome changes for veterans."

ShutDownTheVA@gmail.com

VA Undersecretary for Health David Shulkin said salary constraints, a lengthy hiring process and other factors have limited the agency's ability to attract non-VA applicants.

"We tend to use lots of numbers and that can be confusing, and what I'm trying to do is simplify the message, so here's my message: I need help," Shulkin said. "I need the right leaders to come in and to take these positions of responsibility on behalf of the country, and I don't care if it's 90%, 80%, or 60%. I know I have openings and I don't have the applicants."

USA TODAY scoured hundreds of documents, news accounts and web archives to build a database tracking VA personnel moves since the wait-time scandal broke in 2014, starting with a Phoenix VA facility where 40 veterans had died awaiting care. That case revealed widespread mismanagement of VA facilities and led to McDonald's appointment with a mandate to fix veterans' care.

President Obama has echoed McDonald's pride in the VA's transformation, saying on a recent CNN forum that "we have, in fact, fired a whole bunch of people who are in charge of these facilities." In fact, the VA only moved to fire seven medical center directors. One of them quit and another retired first.

Of the 69 permanent directors installed since McDonald took over, 49 transferred from a different VA medical center, while 12 came from different jobs within the same hospital. The moves included promotions, for instance from associate director to director of a medical center.

In 22 cases, the VA moved directors from one center to another, sometimes to more complex hospitals, but at other times, to less complex facilities. In Ohio, directors in Chillicothe and Columbus simply switched places.

Some of the directors came from facilities where they faced issues ranging from low-ranking quality of care to wait-time falsification to mismanagement identified by outside investigators.

Among them:
• Kathleen Fogarty cut veterans' access to outside care to help overcome a multimillion dollar deficit as director of the Tampa, Fla., VA, in 2011 and repeatedly denied publicly that she was doing it, according to the Tampa Bay Times. In March 2015, the VA transferred her to the director's post at the Kansas City, Mo., VA.

• Joe Battle, who had been the director of the Jackson, Miss, VA, replaced Fogarty in Tampa. The Office of Special Counsel, which investigates whistle-blower claims, concluded in 2013 that Battle had downplayed serious problems with veteran care in Jackson, "calling into question the facility's commitment to implementing serious reforms." During his tenure in Jackson, doctors prescribed narcotics to patients they hadn't seen, schedulers slotted veterans into "ghost clinics" that didn't exist, and the American Legion, two years after he took over, said it was "appalled" by conditions at the facility.

ShutDownTheVA@gmail.com

• Robert Walton went from director of the Harlingen, Texas, VA, to director of the San Antonio VA in November last year. During his tenure in Harlingen, the facility ranked among the lowest in the country in quality and efficiency by the VA's own metrics and investigators found schedulers had routinely falsified veteran wait times under pressure from supervisors.

• Deborah Amdur went from director in White River Junction, Vt., to director of the troubled Phoenix VA last December. In Vermont, the VA's Office of Inspector General found routine scheduling manipulation directed by supervisors and a doctor told investigators that management pressure to increase productivity led to missed cancer diagnoses. Amdur retired in August citing "personal health reasons." Several weeks later, the inspector general released the results of another investigation at the Phoenix VA that found more scheduling improprieties.

• RimaAnn Nelson, who was director of a VA benefits and outpatient clinic in the Philippines, took over for Amdur in Phoenix. She previously had been director of the St. Louis VA when 1,800 veterans were potentially exposed to HIV and hepatitis because of poor sterilization. A follow-up investigation during her tenure found some of the problems hadn't been adequately addressed.

VA officials declined to comment on many of the transfers, citing privacy laws, but said that in general, they were consistent with federal guidelines. They said the vast majority of the moves were promotions. In at least one case, a director requested a transfer for personal

ShutDownTheVA@gmail.com

reasons and the VA approved it.

"You can't have a robust human resource system unless you are providing opportunities for progression," McDonald said. "I'm sure the process we follow for promotion or for transfer to a larger facility is the government-regulated process, which is a fair process dictated by Congress and I'm sure the people who moved to new facilities were, you know, deserved that movement."

VA Secretary Bob McDonald: Veteran wait times not what really matters VA Sec. Bob McDonald regrets uproar over his Disney comment Shulkin said the Phoenix crisis and ensuing media scrutiny triggered an exodus of leaders at the VA, and the agency hasn't been able to attract enough applicants to fill those slots. He said VA officials have filled as many as they could with a mix of inside and outside candidates. Shulkin said there are still more than two dozen directors' jobs open.

They are being filled right now by acting or interim directors, who have cycled through posts frequently at times, destabilizing leadership at some facilities. St. Louis had eight temporary directors between 2013 and this month, when the VA promoted an associate director to fill the role. Los Angeles had four; Oklahoma City and Phoenix had five. Shulkin said one of the issues is salary: Pay for VA medical center directors without specialized medical degrees is capped at $185,100, but in the private sector, the average pay for overseeing a medical center was $349,000, according to 2015 statistics cited by the VA.

ShutDownTheVA@gmail.com

The agency has asked Congress to increase the pay cap, but that effort has stalled on Capitol Hill.

Shulkin said another problem is the federal hiring process, which can take seven months on average for a medical center director and is "heavily weighted" toward applicants with federal government experience. He said he has been working to change that and said three non-VA candidates are currently in the pipeline to take jobs as medical center directors.

"Is it fast enough? No," he said. "Are there enough people responding to my call for assistance? No. But you know I hope somebody reading this might have a reaction that says 'You know what? Maybe I will, maybe I'll consider sending in my CV, this would be a way to give back.'"

VA quit sending performance data to national health care quality site VA to resume sharing quality-of-care data with national consumer site At the Phoenix VA, Shulkin approved Nelson's transfer there because he said she took immediate action to fix problems at her prior posting in St. Louis and he feels comfortable with her leadership skills.

"In my assessment she was an effective leader and the type of leader I need in my toughest place in the country right now, which is Phoenix," he said.

In Tampa, Battle said in a statement that investigators thoroughly reviewed problems at his previous facility in Mississippi. "We addressed any recommendations for improvement and took actions as appropriate," he said, adding that under his leadership, Jackson passed all accreditation reviews on quality of care.

In San Antonio, VA spokeswoman Nenette Madla said the Inspector General and the VA Office of Accountability Review cleared Walton of wrongdoing at his previous post in Harlingen. She did not address quality of care.

Kansas City VA officials did not respond to multiple messages seeking comment on Fogarty's record. Fogarty told The Arizona Republic in 2014 that she balanced the budget at her previous post in Tampa by reducing the amount of time veterans spent in non-VA hospitals.

She also said she has a record of fixing troubled VA facilities during her more than 30 years with the agency.

Amdur could not be reached. She has retired from the VA, and a home number listed for in public records is disconnected. Amdur told The Arizona Republic earlier this year that she was the one who asked the inspector general to investigate wait time manipulation during her tenure in Vermont. "As information from the investigation was revealed, we made changes immediately," she said.

Whatever the case, Phoenix VA whistle-blower Brandon Coleman told USA TODAY that it looks like "bad apples, instead of being fired, are put into other facilities. "And then the VA acts like the problem's solved," he said. "'Nothing else to see here, please move on.'"

ShutDownTheVA@gmail.com

Story #35

2015

New Haley VA director had controversial reign at Mississippi VA hospital[47]

My thanks to The Tampabay Times for permission to reprint this story. www.tampabay.com

Joe D. Battle is expected to take over the James A. Haley VA Medical Center in Tampa, one of the nation's busiest veterans' hospitals, within the next 40 days.

By Times Staff Writer Published Jul. 3, 2015
levesque@tampabay.com

TAMPA — Three years ago, Department of Veterans Affairs manager Joe D. Battle got the unenviable job of turning around the Jackson, Miss., VA hospital, a facility critics called a dysfunctional mess.

---

[47] https://www.tampabay.com/news/military/veterans/new-haley-va-director-had-controversial-history-at-mississippi-hospital/2236089/

The hospital didn't have enough doctors, and two patient deaths were blamed on inadequate staffing. A radiologist was accused of failing to properly read thousands of images. Veterans were assigned to "ghost clinics" without seeing doctors.

"I came here with the goal to build trust in the organization, veterans and anybody in the community to move our hospital beyond the past," Battle told the *Clarion-Ledger* in 2013.

But Battle, appointed last week as the new director of the James A. Haley VA Medical Center in Tampa, ended up fending off his own critics.

They included a VA doctor who accused him of pressuring physicians to permit nurse practitioners to treat patients with little supervision. This whistle-blower also said doctors were asked to sign off on narcotics prescriptions without actually seeing patients, which she said was illegal.

As the U.S. Office of Special Counsel investigated allegations in 2013, Battle called issues at the Jackson VA minor and said they "did not impact patient care."

Someone disagreed: Carolyn Lerner, appointed by President Barack Obama as chief of the OSC, an agency that investigates allegations by federal whistle-blowers.

Lerner said this in a Sept. 17, 2013, report: "Such statements fail to grasp the significance of the concerns raised by (whistle-blowers at the Jackson VA) and call into question

ShutDownTheVA@gmail.com

the facility's commitment to implementing necessary reforms."

Battle, who declined an interview with the *Tampa Bay Times*, is expected to take over the Haley VA, one of the nation's busiest veterans' hospitals, within the next 40 days. He comes to a hospital that has, itself, been in the news, most recently after internal emails showed the facility's kitchens have been infested with rats and cockroaches.

Battle, who has served more than 30 years with the VA, said in a written statement he was "humbled and privileged" to lead Haley.

"Working with my fellow employees, we will build trust and honor (to) those coming through our doors by demonstrating our commitment of caring," he wrote. "I look forward to meeting everyone in the Tampa area veteran community."

Battle took on a big job when he took over the Jackson VA, first as interim director in January 2012 and then as its permanent director that April. Allegations of improper patient care had been widely reported, and the *Associated Press* said Battle "stepped into a public relations nightmare."

The VA has long had a difficult time recruiting doctors to Mississippi. Battle told the U.S. House Veterans Affairs Committee at a 2013 hearing, "Mississippi is a medically underserved state."

The Jackson VA in the years before Battle's arrival came to rely on nurse practitioners — nurses with advanced training

ShutDownTheVA@gmail.com

— in primary-care clinics. That continued under Battle, said one Jackson VA whistle-blower, Dr. Phyllis Hollenbeck.

The OSC said in its September 2013 report that Hollenbeck reported that 85 percent of primary-care patients at the hospital received care from nurse practitioners without being seen by a doctor and that some patients did not know their nurse was not a physician.

Hollenbeck, who did not return a call seeking comment, said she was concerned that nurse practitioners could not provide the same level of care as physicians and that some veterans were, as a result, not being properly diagnosed.

"Dr. Hollenbeck emphasized that these problems persist," Lerner's report said.

In December 2012, Hollenbeck said, she attended a staff meeting with other doctors in which Battle and a regional VA director pressured them to sign "collaborative agreements" with nurse practitioners indicating the physicians were adequately supervising the nurses.

But Hollenbeck said she and others were reluctant to do so because supervision was inadequate. Battle and the second VA official, she said, threatened to withhold 55 percent of doctors' performance pay if they refused.

The doctor said after she and others balked at signing the agreements, Jackson VA nurse practitioners started obtaining licenses to practice from Iowa, where they are not required to have agreements with doctors.

ShutDownTheVA@gmail.com

Hollenbeck also alleged that nurse practitioners were improperly writing prescriptions even though they did not have Drug Enforcement Agency authorization. That practice was eventually ended, she said.

But Hollenbeck said doctors were later asked by supervisors to sign off on prescriptions without seeing the patients, which she said was illegal. She refused.

The hospital, she said, ended up assigning medical residents — physicians in training — to review narcotics prescriptions. "Leadership was telling them to break the law," Hollenbeck said. The VA disagreed.

The agency later said problems at the Jackson VA predated Battle and blamed an "institutional failure" on officials who no longer worked at the hospital.

"The facility's new leadership is taking corrective actions to remedy the past noncompliant practices and prevent them from recurring," the VA said in a Nov. 12, 2013, report to the OSC.

Hollenbeck bristled at that characterization.

"Mr. Joseph Battle in particular cannot be allowed to continue to use the phrase 'These things happened before I came' as a verbal shield," she said. "The same kind of things are still happening. And once you take over command — of a business, medical center, ship or family or any other communal entity — everything is immediately and completely on your watch."

ShutDownTheVA@gmail.com

SUMMARY

ShutDownTheVA@gmail.com

Has the VA harmed you? Here is some advice from lawyersandsettlements.com, which has information on filing a claim and seeking compensation.

Filing a Veteran Medical Negligence Lawsuit[48]

Filing a veterans' medical malpractice claim under the FTCA is complicated and typically requires help from VA medical malpractice lawyers who understand the requirements for filing medical negligence lawsuits. For instance, before you sue, an administrative claim has to be made against the VA for the full amount of damages you have suffered, and that is difficult and risky to determine. Once you have filed your administrative claim, you won't be able to ask for more damages—ever again--unless you have evidence that proves additional damages are warranted and you didn't have knowledge of them prior to filing your claim.

An experienced medical malpractice lawyer can help determine how much in damages you are entitled to receive and will make sure you don't "shortchange" yourself.

After your administrative claim is filed with the FTCA, the VA is entitled to six months for investigation and review of your claim. The VA can then do the following:

48

https://www.lawyersandsettlements.com/lawsuit/veteran_medical_malpractice.html

- Accept the claim and pay it out in full
- Settle the claim for less
- Reject the claim outright.

If your claim is rejected, your next step is to file a lawsuit in federal court. If the VA does nothing within six months, this means that your claim has been rejected. You can sue in federal court under the FTCA, which allows you to file a lawsuit within 2 years of discovering your injury and what caused it. But keep in mind that this timeframe includes the 6-month time period needed to file and complete your administrative claim. It is imperative that you meet these legal deadlines; if not you may lose your claim forever. A veterans' lawyer experienced in VA medical malpractice can help to protect your claim and possible recovery.

VA Legal Malpractice

If you have a VA Medical Malpractice claim, it is important that you work with a lawyer who is experienced and specializes in VA Medical Malpractice. Some veterans have their malpractice cases dismissed because their attorney wasn't experienced with VA issues and procedural requirements for bringing a claim under the FTCA. If your lawyer told you that your VA medical malpractice claim was valid, you may have a *legal malpractice claim* against your lawyer.

A number of VA hospitals have in place an "apology law": administrators and health officials admit their mistakes immediately and negotiate with the victims for extremely low settlements. Although a small settlement can help short-

ShutDownTheVA@gmail.com

term, lawsuit settlements are typically 6 to 28 times greater than what hospitals are offering.

Veteran Medical Malpractice Legal Help

If you are a veteran and have suffered injuries or negligence at a VA hospital, please click the link below to submit your complaint to a veteran malpractice lawyer for a free claim evaluation.

ShutDownTheVA@gmail.com

If you agree that all citizens deserve equal treatment before the law, contact your elected representatives today. Speak up! Make change for the better of all citizens of the world. Comments. Stories? Documents? Send to me.

ShutDownTheVA@gmail.com

Together, we can make a difference.

www.ingramcontent.com/pod-product-compliance
Lightning Source LLC
Chambersburg PA
CBHW030609220526
45463CB00004B/1233